Networking Ahead

Get where you want to go by making powerful, professional connections

Kathy McAfee

3RD EDITION – REVISED AND UPDATED

MOTIVATED PRESS ❯

Networking Ahead: Get where you want to go by making powerful, professional connections
(Third Edition)
Kathy McAfee

Published by Motivated Press
27 Daughtry Court
Travelers Rest, SC 29690
www.MotivatedPress.com

ISBN 978-0-9988032-0-3

Design by Joni McPherson, mcphersongraphics.com

Photography by Matthew J. Wagner

Cartoons by Joe Kohl

Illustration of cupcake by Marissa McAfee

— *Dedication* —

To Byron

from blind date to loving husband,
you are my favorite networking success story.

To those whose stories appear in this book, thank you for
teaching me about the value of networking.

You have enriched my life.

net · work · ing

Function: noun
Date: 1967

The exchange of information or services among individuals, groups, or institutions; specifically: the cultivation of productive relationships for employment or business.

Source: Merriam-Webster Online Dictionary

Contents

Foreword

Networking Ahead is about managing your career and business smarter, smoother, and more productively! As a marketing expert, Kathy McAfee has integrated the wisdom and knowledge gained from her own networking experiences to capture the unique qualities in distinguishing oneself. The process helps to expand the space and shorten the distance to any goal. She illuminates how networking is a powerful tool in becoming the master of one's destiny. Kathy frames the strategies and the tactics in an authentic, user-friendly format.

I loved reading *Networking Ahead* as it provided me with insights about "excellence in building relationships" for multilevel purposes. The personal story format kept my attention while the content focused on how building one's own distinction creates opportunities. By the end, it is evident that the clearer we are about our own personal brand and our unique distinction, the more readily we attract networking opportunities that make inspired contributions in our work as well as in our life.

You will find that *Networking Ahead* is a collection of highly professional, personal, poignant, and profound networking insights organized to create reflections into one's own abilities.

As a business owner and an entrepreneur, I found *Networking Ahead* to have brilliantly packaged up the various know-hows that will increase both the earnings and the "fun factor" in my professional life. And with these insights, you too can take your professional and personal life to new and memorable levels of success.

— Juli Ann Reynolds, President & CEO, Constellation Consulting, and Chair for Vistage

Introduction

Born to Drive

Congratulations on acquiring this book! Whatever means you used to get it—perhaps you bought it, received it as a gift from your employer, a colleague or friend, or checked it out of your local library—it is now yours to enjoy. It is my hope and sincere wish that it will hold your attention long enough so that you may glean a few "golden nuggets" and that these insights will help you to create a more positive trajectory for your professional life.

This book was born through the spirit of networking. All of the stories and ideas within these pages are natural by-products of the networking process. They are derived from people helping people in simple ways that have profound effects. That's networking—the art of building and sustaining mutually beneficial relationships before you need them. And it can have a magical effect on your career, your business, and your life. It's like turbo-charging your car's engine. It gives you more go-power.

My goal in writing this book is to heighten your awareness and increase your motivation toward making networking a key strategy now and for the rest of your life. I want to help you shift into a new gear so that you too can become a motivated networker and acquire the highly prized professional skills of a master connector and the intangible assets of a well-connected person.

> *Networking is the art of building and sustaining mutually beneficial relationships before you need them.*

Learning from My Experience

As a professional speaker and executive presentation coach, I have spent countless hours advising professionals from all disciplines on how they can become the recognized leaders in their fields by mastering the art of high engagement presentations and more effective professional networking. I show them how they can project more of their talent, power, and influence when they present themselves and their ideas to others. It starts with realizing that your value is not just in what you know and what you do, but who you know and who knows you.

Known as America's Marketing Motivator, I'm in the business of pushing people out of their comfort zones and challenging their status quo. I equip and motivate business leaders and entrepreneurs, just like you, to the actions you know deep in your heart and head will push your mission and success forward.

In my seminars and work with business professionals, I often use a car analogy. Driving is an experience we can all relate to. Your network is like the horsepower of a car. A large network will take you farther and faster than a small network. Your network determines the types of goals you can achieve, and how fast you can attain those goals. With a solid professional network in place, you will have greater mobility and access to more and more opportunities for your business and your career.

Your networking ability is like the skill of the driver. A skilled driver, or networker, is comfortable handling obstacles and barriers, driving faster and longer, and avoiding accidents on the way to the destination.

If you have a less powerful car, this book will show you how to build your network and increase your networking skills and confidence. If you have a powerful car, this book will show you how to get the most out of your existing network.

Let's Take a Drive Together

The book is organized into four sections and filled with real life stories as well as practical tactics and tools you can use immediately to improve your business networking. At the end of each section, you will find a checklist to review to ensure you are ready to move on to the next step in our networking journey.

PART I: Ready Your Vehicle – Preparing for Networking Success

Chapters 1 through 7 are devoted to recalibrating your attitude and approach to enable you to network more effectively. We will begin by establishing a compelling reason why you should prioritize networking in your daily business life. We will then start to clear out the roadblocks and limiting beliefs and behaviors that are currently getting in your way to successful networking. Putting a marketing hat on, we will undertake strategic targeting by identifying who really matters in your network and how to increase your frequency of touch with those who matter most. Lastly, we will review the fundamentals of professional image and why you should be more conscious of the first and last impressions that you make with your networking contacts.

PART II: Start Driving – Effective Networking Techniques

Chapters 8 through 13 examine how you can use mirroring and matching techniques to more quickly establish rapport with anyone. You will discover new things about your own personal brand and get permission to express your personal brand while you network. You will develop a stronger 30-second elevator pitch, one that allows you to start more conversations that can lead to more potentially beneficial relationships. The mantra "Think relationships, not transactions; Think conversations, not sales pitches" will be become an integral part of your networking philosophy. We will program in a more efficient follow-up system that will help you cultivate more relationships more easily. And you'll find out why becoming active in your local chamber of commerce and other networking groups is an essential part of your networking drive strategy.

Part III: Accelerate Your Success — Overcome Obstacles and Special Situations

Chapters 14 through 22 outline why and how social media and on-line networking can help you expand your sphere of influence faster for business purposes. You will learn how to work through your existing network to get warm introductions to higher-level prospects and new connections. You will open up your mind to new ways in which you could spend quality time with important people in your network in order to take those relationships further. And you will learn how and when to slow down in order to go the distance with key people and how to navigate around the barriers, human or otherwise.

Part IV: Arriving at Your Destination — Take Your Networking to the Next Level

Chapters 23 through 28 raise your networking game to higher levels, stretching yourself to make more significant connections and to give back to others in more significant ways. You will be nearing the state of unconscious competence, of networking without thinking about it and doing it at higher and higher levels of proficiency. You will be in the graduate level coursework of networking—that is, becoming a master connector—someone who knows many people, who is well connected, and one who can help to create more opportunities for others as well as for yourself.

A Few Special People to Thank

Attorney Judy Gedge, who is now an Associate Professor of Business Law at Quinnipiac University, was a critical cog in the wheel of this book's inception. She was the first person to put the idea of networking as a business topic into my head. She asked me to contribute an article to her *Business Line* newsletter some years back. I went forward to create a one page article, *Perfect Your Pitch: The Most Important Thirty Seconds of Your Business Day.* This was the genesis of my journey into the study of networking. I have been an enthusiastic student ever since. Thanks, Judy!

To the talented Joni McPherson, who designed the cover and interior of this book, as well as my other book, *Stop Global Boring.* In addition to being a gifted graphic designer, Joni is also patient, adaptive, and fast. Thank you, Joni, for your brilliance and continued contributions.

Special thanks to Heather B. Habelka who edited this book. Her expertise with the written word and knowledge of the reader experience made her an outstanding partner on this book.

To my neighbor and friend Ted Fleming, whose strategic eye and generous guidance were paramount to creating a flow structure and tighter focus for this book. No doubt, the reader will appreciate Ted's golden touch as much as I do.

To my friend, Rahna Barthelmess, whose keen marketing sense and abundance of love, support, and encouragement kept me confidently in the driver's seat throughout this project. Rahna—you are most definitely in my Top 50 and have reached the final rung in my networking funnel: friend for life!

To Holly Koziol, the best virtual marketing assistant an author could ever have. Thank you for adding your expertise to this book, and for bringing more joy to my professional life.

To my parents, Roz and Chuck, who not only helped me develop a love of the written word, they have continued to be my cheerleaders and biggest supporters. In fact, my father has served as the chief editor on my blog for the past seven years, and even had a hand in proofreading the manuscript for the third edition of this book.

To my husband Byron, who believed in me, challenged me, kept me on task, and forgave my long hours away from the family and periodic mood swings inherent in an undertaking such as this. You are the best.

Finally, to every single person in my professional network, thank you. I am honored and privileged to know you and to have had the opportunity to help you and to receive your help. As a group, you have taught me so much about networking and business. You make it a joy to participate actively in both.

Pass It On

Ultimately, the value of this book is in the sharing. Whatever you do, don't tuck this book away in your personal library, relegated to a pretty spine graphic among your other books—some read, some not, but all now collecting dust. No. Take this book and pass it on. Share it with other people in your network. We can all get better at this thing called networking and professional relationship building. The very act of sharing this book is a demonstration that you understand the fundamental concepts contained in it and know how to "walk the talk" of networking. It's all about helping others and asking for help.

So without further delay, please turn the page and let's get on with the business of building your professional network.

"The book you don't read won't help."

— JIM ROHN, AMERICAN ENTREPRENEUR, AUTHOR, AND
MOTIVATIONAL SPEAKER (1930-2009)

PART I

Ready Your Vehicle
Preparing for Networking Success

1. You Could Always Take the Bus

The WHY Behind Networking

Can you imagine having to take the bus everywhere you go? Most people in the world have this reality. We lucky folks with access to cars get to drive ourselves where we want to go, when we need to be there. This independence and mobility is really quite a luxury, one that we often take for granted.

I'd like to propose that your personal and professional network is much like that car. It will take you where you want to go, when you need to go there. Without a robust network in place, you will be without wheels, dependent on others or just plain stuck.

What Is Networking, Really?

Networking is essentially about building relationships—one person at a time—actively and systematically cultivating those relationships through time.

Networking is not an event or an activity; it is a strategy for life. Networking is an essential skill for every business and professional person—if not every person—regardless of occupation.

By improving your networking skills and maintaining a robust, healthy professional network of friends, colleagues and acquaintances, you will be able to better manage your career, to influence more positive change in the world, and to build business and professional success for yourself and others.

To do this successfully, I suggest that you follow the advice of Diane Darling, author of *The Networking Survival Guide: Get the Success You Want by Tapping into the People You Know*. She says, "Networking is the art of building and sustaining mutually beneficial relationships." I'd like to add "before you need them" so that they are in place when you do need them. That's the value of networking.

But wait a minute.

Why Network? You Already Have a Job

Networking is most commonly associated with job-seeking. It's what you do when you've been laid off, downsized, or fired and need to find gainful new employment fast. It's a dreaded activity for most people, especially when they haven't stayed in touch with people they've worked with in the past, and now it's time to make those awkward phone calls.

They go something like this:

> "Hello, John. This is Kathy. Do you remember me? We used to work together at XYZ company. Sorry that I haven't been in touch lately. Sorry that I didn't return your phone calls when you got laid off. It's just that I was really busy on that project. Anyway, I've just been laid off and I need your help."

The calls may not go exactly like this, but they are uncomfortable and very hard to make. They are also interesting to receive. But you've got to make those calls. Your livelihood is at stake.

Now imagine what that call would sound like, feel like, and be like if you had stayed in regular touch with your past colleagues? Perhaps they would even call you once they heard the news. Would they be more willing to offer you assistance and support? Chances are, yes they would.

Networking for Career Management

Networking is a critical component of good career management. It is something you do throughout your work life, when you are working and when you are not. If it helps you to do it, think of it as "network or not work." By having a robust professional network, you will be able to weave and bob and change jobs, career paths, and start entrepreneurial ventures more easily. Your supporters will be behind you. They will be connected with you. They will know what your dreams and goals are. If you practice ongoing networking and good relationship management skills, they will help you solve your career challenges.

Why Network? You Already Know Everyone

Some of you may feel that you have plenty of friends, and your need to add more is not that pressing. Who has the time to make new friends and maintain new friendships? My life is full as it is!

Part of what makes life rich and full is the presence of good relationships, true friendships, and strong connections. Money comes and goes, jobs come and go, and yes, some relationships come and go too. Your ability to develop a pipeline of good connections will help you maintain your happiness, wealth, and opportunities, and create positive influence in the world.

Networking for Greater Personal Influence

Think about networking from a personal influence point of view. Imagine what good you could do in the world if you have more supportive people on your side. What are you passionate about, and what changes do you want to see in your community, your country, your world? What non-profit organizations are you committed to helping? What causes and social or environmental problems ignite your fire? By sharing these personal passions and convictions with others in your personal and professional network, you can affect more change.

Here's a story of how it worked for me recently. I met a woman entrepreneur for a networking coffee. She was a health coach who was trying to figure out how to go to market with her brand and her unique services and philosophy. In the course of our networking discussion, I shared some personal information that I was a foster parent and was hoping to adopt the two boys living with us. She immediately latched onto this and began to ask me many questions. She and her family had been thinking of adopting a child, but didn't know where to go or how to begin the process. As a result of our conversation, she and her husband signed up for a foster care orientation class and within one year had a 2-year-old girl living in their family. Imagine how I felt when I received the adoption announcement card from her family? Networking had once again produced magic in the world and had changed the lives of other people for good. That's what I call personal influence.

Why Network? You're Not in Sales or Marketing

Some people think that networking only serves those folks who are responsible for business development or sales and marketing. If your specialty lies in a different area, why would you be concerned about networking since you are not responsible for generating new business opportunities?

The answer is because you can. You can have an impact on the business by leveraging the people you know. You can help your organization solve problems better, faster, or cheaper by accessing the expertise of the people in your professional network. You may even be the unexpected one who introduces your organization to a major growth opportunity by connecting new people with new ideas. You potentially have special power if you learn to harness your professional network.

> *Your ability to develop a pipeline of good connections will help you maintain your happiness, wealth, and opportunities, and create positive influence in the world.*

I was invited to speak to a networking group focused on technology startups. I was speaking alongside a woman named Merrie of SBIR, Small Business Innovation Research, a government funded program that I had not heard of before this. I took the opportunity to call Merrie before the event and introduce myself. We got to know each other over the phone, and when we arrived at the night of the event, rapport was already established.

After that event, Merrie and I stayed in touch. She introduced me to the world of high technology startups and showed me how her team at SBIR was matchmaking inventors and innovators with large companies in order bring to market great ideas that could change the way we solve problems in the environment, health care, national defense/security, and more. This was a whole new world to me and one that I hadn't considered serving until I met Merrie.

Merrie and her boss Deb have hired me to speak three times at their regional and national SBIR conferences. I have met hundreds of brilliant innovators who want to take their great ideas and create commercial success. As it turns out, inventors also need to improve their networking and presentation skills. My half-day workshops "Perfect Your Pitch" have been very popular at the conferences and have changed the way many of these technical professionals communicate and present their ideas.

This story illustrates how business opportunities can be created, not only for you but for others, as the new connections, new ideas and new inspirations cascade across many spheres of influence. Imagine what business opportunities you might spur on by improving your networking skills.

Now that you understand the "why" behind networking, it's time to examine the things that will try to get in your way. The next chapter explores some of the physical, mental, and emotional roadblocks that will slow you down, and how you can overcome them.

> *"Now here comes the big ones. Relationships! We all got 'em; all want 'em. What do we do with 'em?"*
> — JIMMY BUFFET IN HIS SONG FRUITCAKES

2. Clear the Roadblocks

Things that Get in Your Way

ROADBLOCK NO. 1: **Social Reluctance**

Networking for Introverts, Shy Guys and Gals

Networking does not come naturally for most people. In fact, it can be quite terrifying to walk into a room full of people you don't know. There can be moments of reluctance even for the most outgoing extravert. Fears, hesitations, doubt, and awkwardness well up inside us to such heightened levels that it becomes a significant emotional event. We don't like it, so as a defensive measure, we avoid it. I call this social reluctance.

This is especially challenging for people who identify themselves as introverts by nature or those who are shy. You may already know that shyness and introversion are not the same thing. Introversion is a personality trait that usually lasts a lifetime. Shyness, on the other hand, is an emotional state that can be overcome.

Carol Bainbridge, who writes about shyness and introversion, suggests that while an introvert may also be shy, introversion itself is not shyness. Basically, an introvert is a person who is energized by being alone or with one or two people at most. Being in crowds of people (e.g., parties, conventions, networking meetings) literally exhausts that person. Have you ever felt that way?

Are You an Introvert?

Ms. Bainbridge explains, "Introverts are more concerned with the inner world of the mind. They enjoy thinking, exploring their thoughts, and exploring their feelings. They often avoid social situations because being around people drains their energy. This is true even if they have good social skills. After being with people for any length of time, such as at a party, they need time alone to recharge."

If this description fits you, you may be an introvert, and that's perfectly fine. Networking and relationship building are not the exclusive dominion of extroverts. If you are an introvert, you too can be successful with people, relationships and yes, networking. You will do so in a way that works best for you. Just keep reading.

Are You Shy?

When I was in college, I had the privilege of sitting in the classroom with the brilliant and charismatic professor, Philip Zimbardo, Ph.D., of Stanford University. His psychology classes were "standing room only." Shy or not, many of us attended his lectures because the topic, quite frankly, was vitally important to our futures (not to mention our weekends).

In his groundbreaking book *Shyness: What It Is. What to Do About It.* Dr. Zimbardo reveals that shyness is pervasive, with as many as 40 percent of people in his research study considering themselves shy. If you're shy, you are not alone. There are millions of shy people all around us.

> *Networking and relationship building are not the exclusive dominion of extroverts. If you are an introvert, you too can be successful with people.*

Shy on the Outside—Torn Up on the Inside

Dr. Zimbardo's study presented a surprising portrait of those with the shy condition. Their mild-mannered exterior conceals roiling turmoil inside. The shy disclosed that they are excessively self-conscious;

constantly sizing themselves up negatively and overwhelmingly preoccupied with what others think of them. While everyone else is meeting and greeting, they are developing plans to manage their public impression (If I stand at the far end of the room and pretend to be examining the painting on the wall, I'll look like I'm interested in art and won't have to talk to anybody). They are consumed by the misery of the social setting (I'm having a horrible time at this party because I don't know what to say and everyone seems to be staring at me). All the while their hearts are pounding, their pulses are speeding, and butterflies are swarming in their stomach—physiological symptoms of genuine distress.

Being shy can be extremely uncomfortable, if not emotionally painful. Check out Dr. Zimbardo's website: shyness.com for tons of up-to-date information, surveys to complete, scales, and more to help shy folks overcome their social reluctance with confidence.

An Unusual Case of Narcissism

Mark Shepard, master practitioner and trainer of Neuro Linguistic Programming (NLP), the study of how you run your brain, believes that shyness is a form of narcissism, a trait where a person is overly concerned with self-image and ego. Shepard, a recovered "shy guy" himself, works with shy people to help them clear their limiting beliefs and negative emotions. His program "Clear the Fear" helps shy people and others learn how to get out of themselves and get comfortable conversing and connecting with other people. He even wrote a song about it. It's hysterical.

Here are a few lyrics from Mark Shepard's song *Narcissism:*

Narcissism, narcissism
you know you're really living
When you're looking through the prism of good ole narcissism
If you want to get ahead in life you better get this right
People don't want to hear about you

They want you to hear about *them*!
Narcissism, narcissism
you know you're really living
When you're looking through the prism of good ole narcissism
What I've thought about you is all wrong
It's been all about me all along
And what I think about you is all about me
So we might as well sing this song…Together!

Shared with permission. © 1998-2010 by Mark Shepard All Rights Reserved. For more inspiring and entertaining songs, go to MarkShepardSongs.com

The good news is that shyness can be overcome. In fact, practicing networking and learning the skills of conversation can be an excellent way to get rid of the shyness problem. Like any learned skill, it will be uncomfortable at first, but after time, you will get good at it. With networking, you also experience extra benefits: you make new friends and get more opportunities. Why stay trapped inside your narcissistic shy self, when you can come out and play with the rest of us? Once free of your shyness, you will never look back.

How Can You Do it More Comfortably?

My advice to introverted and shy people is to keep in mind that networking is nothing more than building relationships one at a time. Your energy and focus should be on one person at a time. Find ways and venues that allow you to maintain your personal energy and interest. This book will give you new ideas on just how you can do that.

"The way you overcome shyness is to become so wrapped up in something that you forget to be afraid."
— CLAUDIA "LADY BIRD" JOHNSON, WIFE OF US PRESIDENT LYNDON B. JOHNSON (1912 - 2007)

ROADBLOCK NO. 2: **Comfort Zone**
Hanging Out with People You Already Know

To be an effective networker you must continually meet new people and add them to your professional network. Just hanging out with the people you already know is not going to grow your sphere of influence. Imagine if you had adopted this limiting attitude when you were in elementary school? You'd only know the people in your third grade class. Not good.

Life has a way of pushing us out of our comfort zones. We move to new places, attend new schools, work for different companies, drive on new roads. In fact, it's really hard not to meet new people. So unless you are in the witness protection program, go ahead, put yourself out there, extend your hand and meet new people. It's good for you.

But for some reason, meeting new people in the context of networking takes on a whole new level of hesitation. It can create the same physiological response as public speaking (and we know how some of you feel about doing that). Ultimately, it's fear and uncertainty that stops you.

This reminds me of a personal story when I experienced extreme levels of hesitation that resulted in hermit-like behavior. When I was in sixth grade my family moved to a new community, which meant a new school for me. It was toward the end of the school year, but still it was traumatizing for a young girl whose whole life was built around her old friends, her old school, and her old neighborhood. I was somebody there, a big shot. Now, I would have to start all over again. It was exhausting just thinking of it.

> *The next time you find yourself declining to attend a conference or networking meeting, ask yourself: "What am I afraid of?"*

So I stayed in my room for a full three months after moving to the new house. I didn't go outside and play with new kids. I went to my room immediately after school every day. During the summer, I stayed inside where it was safe. I practically missed the entire summer. I was pissed off, sad, scared, lonely, and becoming a bit depressed. The babysitter didn't notice.

Then the new school year started, and I was forced to come out of my shell. It was a new year and new school (junior high school now) for everyone. We were all in the same boat. Everyone had to make new friends. I was forced out of my comfort zone. My self-induced, extended pity party was officially over. Thank goodness, as I could now get on with the business of living and learning.

So what do you have in common with a twelve-year-old girl who was traumatized by a changed environment? You're not twelve, you may not even be a girl, but no doubt you too have experienced something like this in your life. It's an imaginary roadblock that becomes quite real and powerful and can be personally and professionally disabling.

So the next time you find yourself declining to attend a conference or networking meeting, ask yourself: "What am I afraid of?" or "What's the worst thing that could happen to me?" Better yet, ask yourself, "What's the best thing that could happen to me?"

It's time to come outside and play, make new friends, and create new opportunities. President Franklin Roosevelt said, "There is nothing to fear but fear itself." He had a point.

> *"Don't be afraid to expand yourself, to step out of your comfort zone. That's where the joy and the adventure lie."*
> — HERBIE HANCOCK, AMERICAN PIANIST, BANDLEADER, AND COMPOSER

ROADBLOCK NO. 3 **Lazy and Undisciplined**

The Shortest Path to Mediocrity

- -

I'm going to hit you hard here. Networking takes effort. It takes personal discipline. It takes commitment and follow through. Most of us are just too lazy, undisciplined, or disorganized to do it well. We start, and then we stop. We do it for a while, and then we quit. If something bad happens (e.g., get laid off from the job), we quickly start networking again. It's as if networking is behind a glass case that reads, "In case of emergency, break open."

Networking for the Health of It

Networking is like exercise and eating right. Exercise regularly, eat nutritious foods, sleep well, limit the toxins, and you may just keep yourself out of the hospital. You'll look better and feel better. You'll potentially live longer and live better.

With effort, it will become your new lifestyle, an automatic daily routine. You'll wonder how you ever lived without doing it. But most of us would rather take a pill, go through surgery, or just live a fat, high-risk life than put exercise and healthy living into our daily routines. Crazy, isn't it?

Protecting Your Greatest Assets

"Anything worth having is worth working for," some wise person once said. Yes, your health is worth it. It is your greatest asset. Without your health, you will be severely limited. It's a game changer. Ask anyone who's run the cancer gauntlet.

After your health, your next greatest asset, I propose, is the quality of your relationships. Think about the special people in your life who make living rich and meaningful for you. What are you doing to protect these assets? Are you investing time and effort in those relationships?

Or ignoring them and taking them for granted? Be honest.

Relationships are at the very heart of networking. They are the big prize in networking. Long-term, mutually beneficial relationships are what you are working toward. Therefore, it only makes sense that some effort will be required to create them and to maintain them. When it comes to relationships, lazy doesn't last long. Couch potatoes don't make good husbands (or wives for that matter), nor do they make good friends or good contacts.

What's so cool about this roadblock is that it is 100 percent in your control. You can do something about it. You don't need external solutions to put it into play. Just add effort and sustain it over a period of time until it becomes a personal habit. Discipline yourself, and make networking and relationship building a daily priority in your life. If you do this, you'll feel better. More people will care about you. You will care about more people. This is good.

> *"You can't teach people to be lazy—either they have it, or they don't."*
>
> — DAGWOOD BUMSTEAD, THE MAIN CHARACTER IN THE LONG-RUNNING COMIC STRIP *BLONDIE*

ROADBLOCK NO. 4 **Shortage of Time**

How Are You Using Your 86,400 Seconds Per Day?

"There's not enough time in the day." Don't you love this excuse? It is indisputable. Everyone has the same problem. The busier we get, the more important we feel. How cool is that?

This is not so cool if it keeps you from doing what's imporant in your life. Never forget that your *To Do* list is not the same as your priorities list. Not all tasks are equally important. We have choices. Not just excuses.

Let me share a story that changed how I view time. It was shared to me by the head of my martial arts academy instructor, Grand Master Yu, who is a Judo Olympian, and an eighth-degree black belt in Tae Kwon Do, Judo, and Hapkido. He is on the council of the World Korean Judo Society. Clearly, he is an influential man in the global community of martial arts and has positively impacted many lives in his 30-plus years of running martial arts schools, including mine.

One day, when I was feeling particularly overwhelmed (and apparently showing it to others with my body language and energy), he took me aside and told me a story in his charming Korean accent that I have grown to love during my studies with him. He said:

> "Let's say, I give you a thousand dollars every day. You can spend it as you wish. What you do not spend, you must give back to me. Next day, I will give you another thousand dollars. You spend it as you wish. What you do not spend, you must return to me. Next day, the same thing. [pause] Tell me, how will you spend the money?
>
> [pause]
>
> Now, instead of a thousand dollars, I give you 24 hours. I give you 24 hours each day. You spend it as you like. What

you don't spend, I take back at end of day. Next day, I give you another 24 hours. Next day, you get another 24 hours. [pause] Question: how will you spend your time?"

I was dumbfounded, speechless, and utterly transformed with this story. I realized that I get this precious, valuable, and seemingly unending gift of time. A fresh supply of time—24 hours every day! That's 1,440 minutes each day or 86,400 seconds each day. Wow! If that were money, I'd be rich!

But unlike money, you can't save time. You can't accumulate it and get compounding interest on it. You can't put it in a bank account, invest it in the market and hope that it grows. Time comes as quickly as it goes. When it's gone, it's gone. But you do get a lot of it, and you have choices as to how you use it.

I tell you this personal story so that you too may adopt a new attitude about time. This is your opportunity to stop making excuses about time and start embracing it as a gift.

While there will always be pressures and demands on your time, ultimately it is yours. You choose how you spend it. Why not spend a little time each day on building and maintaining relationships? That, my friend, will pay you rewarding dividends.

> "We realize our dilemma goes deeper than shortage of time; it is basically a problem of priorities. We confess, we have left undone those things that ought to have done; and we have done those things which we ought not to have done."
> — Charles-Camille Saint-Saëns, French composer (1835–1921)

ROADBLOCK NO. 5 **Techno-Phobic Versus Techno-Addict**
Misusing Technology to Your Detriment

Is technology your friend or foe when it comes to networking and relationship building? Imagine living without your iPhone or Galaxy. Was there life before Facebook, LinkedIn, or Twitter? Of course there was. More advances in technology will be introduced after this book is published and will continue to be introduced on a daily basis.

How Do You Keep Up with All of It?

The good news is that we human beings are learning machines. Even as we age, our brains continue to make new neurological connections, our bodies regenerate, and we can learn new skills and tasks. But for some of us, the learning process involves a fair amount of complaining.

Technology-Life Balance

In order to strike a healthy balance in using technology to enhance your relationships, you'll want to keep a few things in mind:

- **Technology is not going away.** It continues to evolve, and you must evolve with it. If you bury your head in the sand and decide that you are not going to participate in social media, for example, you will become outdated quickly. Your skills, knowledge, and experience will also become dated.

> *Because networking is fundamentally about relationships, you must reveal the real you—online and off. Anything else would be phony, exhausting, and ultimately unsustainable.*

- **Technology is your servant, not your master.** Like any tool, technology is only as good as your ability to use it, understand it, and control it. "Use the right tool for the right job," my husband reminds me when we are tackling home and garden projects. When networking and relationship building, remember that technology creates new communication channels—additional ways of staying in touch with the people that you care about. But don't let technology alter the fundamental ways in which you relate to other people.

- **Technology only temporarily hides your flaws.** The song "I'm So Much Cooler Online" from country singer Brad Paisley reminds us of how easy it is to appear to be something you are not when you present yourself on social media. Because networking is fundamentally about relationships, you must reveal the real you—online and off. Anything else would be phony, exhausting, and ultimately unsustainable.

Moving On

These are just some of the known roadblocks. You might encounter others. Your job as a motivated networker is to find ways to go around, under, or over them, and find a working detour. There are people who need to meet you; people you can help and who can help you to achieve your goals. In the next chapter, we'll take a look at who really matters in your network, and how you can become more targeted and purposeful with your networking strategy.

> *"Yes, I love technology, but not as much as you, you see. But I still love technology. Always and forever."*
> — KIP'S WEDDING SONG FROM THE MOVIE *NAPOLEON DYNAMITE*

3. What Road to Take?

Who Really Matters in Your Network

So many roads, so little time. When it comes to networking, everybody is a potential new connection for you. You never know who could bring value into your life. It's mind-boggling to think of all the time you could spend meeting new people and developing these new relationships. And while I believe everyone has value, I believe we must strive to be targeted in our approach to networking.

The reality is that you have a limited amount of time and energy. Since networking is not your full-time job, it's time to figure out who is most important to you and with whom you will invest more of your time, energy and talent in developing a lasting relationship.

Who Is in Your World?

No doubt you know many people from different areas of your life. You work with some, you play with some, and you serve on committees with some. The question is: How many people do you know, who know you? The average for most people is around 250. Perhaps you know a few less; perhaps you know a few more.

My World Exercise™

Think of the people you have met and who know you. List them by the different groups that you associate them with:

- Family
- Friends
- Neighbors
- Work colleagues

- Clients
- Past job associates
- Exercise/fitness groups
- Church or spiritual communities
- Community service or volunteer groups
- Hobbies
- College friends
- School/kids/scouts/sports

You can download a free template of the "My World Exercise" worksheet at americasmarketingmotivator.com/my-world/

I recommend that you first do this exercise without access to your computer database or phone. You will probably be able to generate a list of several hundred people. Once you have that list, access your address lists loaded on your cell phone, computer, and social media sites and look over the holiday cards that you've sent and received in the past. Watch how the list of people that you know grows. How many people are on your list now? Are you surprised? This is a glimpse at who is in your current network. Keep this list handy.

Who Is in Your Inner Circle?

What do all these people have in common? You. You are the connecting thread, the link to all these people. They are in your life and in your sphere of influence.

Now, I'd like you to think in pictures. Imagine a ring of concentric circles, like the logo for the Target store or a bull's-eye target for an archer. Seen from a networking point of view, the common center point is you. Yes, you are the center of the universe!

Surrounding you and your center point is a small group of people who matter most to you. They love you and care for you and would do anything for you. Who could you share your biggest dreams, fears, concerns and triumphs with? Who would give you candid, critical

feedback, even when you didn't ask for it? Who comes to mind when you read this description? Perhaps members of your family or your best friends? Write their names down.

Now think a little more broadly about the people closest to you in your career/work life. With whom do you have a good relationship? Who would call you back promptly if you left a voice mail? Who would go out of the way to help you out if you asked? Who do you respect, admire, and care about? Write their names down.

Your Top 50 Contacts

What you have begun to build is the list of your Top 50 contacts—the 50 most important people in your network. I support the idea that our personal and professional networks cross over. In fact, my mother, father, husband, uncle, and sisters-in-law have helped me achieve my professional goals many times over. Why would I exclude them? They care the most for me of anyone I know.

In making my list of my Top 50 networking contacts, I have five basic criteria that I like to meet. You may have more qualifying factors, but here are some simple guidelines you might consider:

1. You have a good relationship with this person.

2. You care about this individual as a person.

3. This individual cares about you as a person.

4. You can help this person achieve his or her goals.

5. This person can help you achieve your goals.

Now, with these criteria in mind, who comes to mind as members of your Top 50 networking contacts? Note: you can write them down in any order. Hierarchy is not important.

So what do you do with your Top 50 contact list when you create it? You make these relationships a priority by putting more time and attention into them. I recommend you practice a higher frequency of touch with these important people.

Top 50 Contacts

{ *Quality of communication counts when you are networking with your Top 50 contacts.* }

50-5-10-2 Strategy

This strategy was shared with me by Angelo Rossetti, an avid networking and tennis professional. In 2008 Angelo and his identical twin brother, Ettore, broke the world record for the longest tennis rally, successfully completing 25,944 consecutive strokes during a period of 14 hours and 31 minutes. (Now that's bladder control!)

Personally I do love the game of tennis, and I admire the amazing feat of the Rossetti brothers. More importantly, Angelo taught me a great deal about effective networking. One of his ideas that stuck with me was the idea of knowing who my Top 50 contacts are and practicing the 50-5-10-2 strategy.

Here's how it works:

- **50:** Identify your Top 50 contacts.

- **5:** Reach out and touch base with them once every five weeks or so.

- **10:** That means you will be reaching out to 10 people per week.

- **2:** That equals two people per day (Monday to Friday; you can take the weekend off).

Can you do that? Touch base with two people each day? And not just any two people—two people who are among the most important to you in your professional network. If you commute, consider reaching out to one person during your morning commute and one person on your afternoon commute. This assumes that you can speak on the phone safely while you drive.

Find out which communication channels your Top 50 folks prefer. Are they telephone people? E-mail people? Texting people? Do they like to sit down with you for coffee or lunch? Are they golfing people? Quality of communication counts when you are networking with your Top 50 contacts.

Expanding Your Sphere of Influence

One of the benefits of becoming a motivated networker is that you are continually expanding your sphere of influence. This means you are involved and have a say in how the world works—at least part of it. You have broader resources that you can draw upon when you need help. The more people you know and who know you will determine how many people show up at your funeral—or your 100th birthday—whichever comes first.

Let's bring back the image of those concentric circles now. What are the next rings that lie outside those of your Top 50 contacts? I propose that there are three more rings that we need to address here in our work together: Active, Lost, and Future Networks.

Your Sphere of Influence

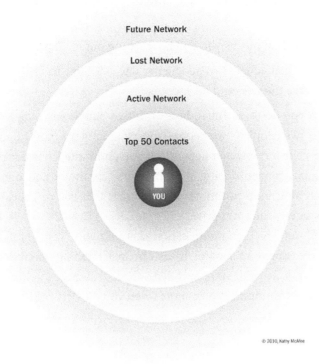

Future Network

Lost Network

Active Network

Top 50 Contacts

YOU

© 2010, Kathy McAfee

- **Active Network.** These are the people in your daily world. You live next door to them, you work with them, and you see them at your meetings and gatherings. You may be friends, acquaintances, or even arch-enemies. The point is, you run into them regularly. They are "active" in your life right now, and you have some kind of relationship with them. These are the easiest relationships to develop and strengthen from a networking point of view. Why? Proximity and regularity. You only have to extend yourself a little bit to start to build upon these relationships.

- **Lost Network.** These are the people who used to be in your active network, but something changed, and you haven't seen them in a very long time. You used to live next door to them, you were best friends in school, you worked on that project together at the old company, you socialized with them and then—something happened. Someone moved, someone got divorced, someone left the company, and you lost touch with that person. You haven't seen each other in a very long time. You may not even remember that person's full name. The good news is that you can reclaim your lost network by finding those individuals on social media. Just recently, I was contacted by my best friend in middle school. It had been years since we were in touch with each other. It was a joy to hear about her life and family and her many adventures through the years. We can now pick up where we left off. This relationship may become important again in my life and business. Or it may just be a wonderful blast from the past. Either way, good stuff.

- **Future Network.** These are all the people you haven't yet met, but would like to. You may discover them purely by accident or chance (the power of serendipity). Other people may suggest them as good contacts for you, or you might purposefully seek them out through your networking activity. This is what I call "targeted networking." Think about whom you would like to add to your professional network right now. Whom would you like to have a relationship with that could add value to your life, career, and business? Whose company would you enjoy and whom would you like to learn from? Whose brain would you like to pick? Write that person's name down.

If you are drawing a complete blank right now, don't worry; this is a normal reaction to this exercise. Why not get some ideas by flipping through a business magazine, newspaper, or published list of people in your industry? Who are the movers and shakers in your field? Pick one, do your research on that person (that's easy these days thanks to the Internet and social media). Now, find someone in your existing network (Top 50 Contacts or Active) who knows that person or knows someone else who knows that person and would be willing to introduce you. How do you make that happen? Just tell everyone you know whom you are looking to meet.

A few years back I had the pleasure of conducting a series of two-day workshops called "Powerful Presentations." A number of executives from the insurance and financial services industries attended my course. They were all dynamic, talented, and motivated leaders very willing to try new things to sharpen their presentation skills and confidence. One such leader was Alan. Shortly after the training workshop, Alan had a team presentation with the C-suite executives at his company, a leading global financial services organization. He and I had a private coaching session to strategize his team's approach. He committed to doing his Six Sigma update presentation completely without PowerPoint, using props and stories to enhance audience engagement.

Alan e-mailed me after his team presentation with the great news that it had gone extremely well. The CEO loved it and suggested that Alan and his team take this show on the road. Needless to say I was jumping up and down in my office after reading Alan's e-mail. At that moment, I set the goal to meet the CEO of this large financial services organization.

For the next eight months I told many people about my goal to meet the CEO, not knowing who might know her or have connections to her. I did try the direct approach, asking Alan for an introduction, but that didn't materialize as I had hoped. Then I tried cold-calling the CEO's office. Like most vendors, I was quickly referred to the HR department. No luck through this route.

I incorporated my goal of meeting this CEO into almost every professional networking talk that I gave. I used it as an example of how the more specific you are in who you are looking to meet, the closer you will get to make that connection. It wasn't until I sat down one day and had lunch with Judith, a wonderful woman in my Top 50, that I moved closer to my goal. At that time, Judith led the development team of the YWCA Hartford Region. In the course of our conversation, I shared my goal of meeting this CEO and asked Judith if she knew her. She told me she had lunch with her the week before. Wow! I was one degree away. Now I had to ask the big question, "Judith, do you think you could introduce me to her? I'd like to network with her and do more business with her company."

Judith said that she could do that, but suggested a better strategy. "Why don't we introduce you first to Liz, who used to work directly for the CEO and who is still very good friends with her? Liz is involved with some YWCA projects, as are you, and I think you two would hit it off. Liz can then make the introduction."

I followed Judith's advice and got to know Liz, who, by the way, is a dynamic, talented, motivated, and fun person. Liz is now part of my active network—a real bonus that I wasn't expecting to have on this journey!

Over the next two months, I had several face-to-face exchanges with Liz, getting to know her in the context of our board work together with the YWCA. She even purchased my audio program entitled "Motivated Networking Follow-up" that I was offering as a fundraising project for the non-profit organization.

I ran into Liz at the sponsor breakfast of the YWCA's "Money Conference for Women." She enthusiastically came up to me at the breakfast buffet line and said, "I am so impressed with you. You're the reason I'm here today. Come sit down next to me." We had a great conversation over scrambled eggs and fruit. I then took a deep breath and asked her the question: "Liz, do you think you could introduce me to your CEO?" She responded by pounding her fist on the table and saying "Consider it done!"

Two months later, the CEO, Liz, and I were having lunch together in the company cafeteria. It was relaxed and interesting. As it turns out, the CEO is a very approachable and real person who happens to have a very big job. I followed up after that luncheon with a personalized card.

Three months later, I got an e-mail from an HR leader at the company regarding an executive coaching assignment. Upon probing, it turned out that the CEO had suggested my name. I landed the assignment and now have the opportunity once again to serve the company and its employees. Networking builds not only relationships, but also real business opportunities!

What's the moral of this story? Decide who you want to add to your professional network, tell everyone in your active network whom you are looking to meet, and then be ready when the opportunity presents itself. It will present itself if you are patient, flexible, and have the ability and willingness to build strong, supportive relationships.

Now that you know who is important in your network and how to expand your sphere of influence, we will move on to examining what I call the true spirit of networking. The concepts in this next chapter are powerful enough to change networking from a dreaded activity to a joyful experience.

> *"Treasure your relationships, not your possessions."*
> — ANTHONY J. D'ANGELO, COLLEGIATE EMPOWERMENT

4. Rules of the Road

Embrace the True Spirit of Networking

The roads are shared by people in all types of vehicles: SUVs, sedans, sports cars, wagons, motorcycles, bicycles, trucks, buses, etc. We also share our roads with pedestrians and sometimes wildlife. We must observe the rules of the road in order to navigate safely and get where we need to be.

The same holds true for networking, but the rules of the road are mostly unwritten. They include giving, sharing, caring, and reciprocating.

Helping Others; Asking for Help

To me, this is the true spirit of networking. It is about helping others to solve problems and achieve their goals, professionally and personally. And, it's about asking for help from others. You too have problems and dreams that require attention and help. When you approach your networking with an attitude of helpfulness, you will accelerate your success and make faster and more meaningful connections with people.

Many people I know (mostly women) are excellent at helping others, but lousy at asking for help for themselves. To be an effective networker, you must be able to do both: help others and ask for help for yourself.

My good friend Kim once complained to me that she always extended herself to others in networking, and there was never any reciprocation. To her, it felt like a one-way giving street. I asked her, "So, how good are you at asking for help from others?" She was silent and gave me a look that told me, "You're right. I stink at that."

Let's face it, it takes a strong person to ask for help—to reach out to others and share gaps and needs that you might otherwise want to keep to yourself. In college, I learned that the smartest students were the ones who asked for help, who looked for additional resources, human and otherwise. It took me quite a few semesters of struggling on my own to realize that I was surrounded by a wealth of resources.

Sometimes the best way to help yourself is to ask for help from others. The key to asking for help in networking is knowing what you want and whom you are looking to meet. You must get fairly specific about this. And you must bring this up during your networking meetings and conversations. Your contacts can't read your mind, and if you don't bring the subject up, it may go unnoticed and unrealized. And whose fault is that?

Giver's Gain Philosophy

Dr. Ivan Misner, founder and chairman of the BNI network, the self-proclaimed largest business networking organization and referral network, is credited for the "giver's gain" idea: You must give of yourself freely and without expectation of return for your giving. If you do this, good things will come your way.

I call this the boomerang effect. Cast out good things in the world, and good things will come back to you, perhaps not immediately, but eventually. Send out negative energy and negative actions into the world and you know what's coming back? Eventually, bad things come your way. You get what you give. You reap what you sow.

The key to asking for help in networking is knowing what you want and whom you are looking to meet.

Law of Reciprocity

The law of reciprocity means to give and take mutually—to return in kind. It is often associated with the expression "You scratch my back, I'll scratch yours." When someone gives you something or does a kindness for you, you feel an internal obligation to repay the favor in some way. Giving and receiving favors are common daily exchanges among friends, which happen in every culture on earth.

Of course, the law of reciprocity is more carefully guarded when practiced in the context of business or politics, where "buying favors" can not only produce negative public opinion but sometimes legal consequences. Most companies have "gift policies" and discourage their employees, leaders, and board members from receiving things of value from others. Even if the thing has no value, the act of receiving it may be misconstrued by others. This is to be avoided at all costs. No company likes to deal with this sort of publicity embarrassment—it drives up PR costs and creates an unneeded company distraction.

So how do you resolve this issue when the very definition of networking is: the art of building and maintaining mutually beneficial relationships before you need them? Giving, taking, and exchanging are part of what happens when people who care about each other try to help each other. Is it really necessary to have our guard up all the time? Is it wise to avoid receiving favors from others because you don't want to feel obligated, guilty, or beholden to anyone else?

I'd like to give you another way to think about this. Practice giving of yourself with no strings attached. Whether it's your time, money, possessions, or knowledge, give without expectation of return. I know that this is a tough thing to do. We at least expect to get a thank you (verbal or written). But let that go too. Practice giving for the sheer love of it—because it makes you feel good. When you get good at that, then you are ready to practice receiving with grace. Allow other people to give to you because it brings them joy. Whether it is a compliment, treating you to lunch, giving you a book or some helpful advice, just receive it gracefully.

I have a dear friend named Gary. He was my very first boyfriend in high school (feels like a million years ago). He is married to a wonderful woman named Denise, and they have two lovely kids. Every Christmas, Gary and Denise send a small present to a group of 15 friends. Year after year, they send something inexpensive, but fun and spirited. Their gift makes us smile, and receiving Gary and Denise's gift has become part of our holiday tradition. I decided a long time ago that I was going to practice the act of receiving gracefully without the expectation of immediate reciprocation. I send a thank-you card and let them know that we received it and enjoyed it. But I don't rush off to the store to buy them something because I feel guilty. I just enjoy the good feelings of receiving someone's kindness. I believe Gary and Denise do what they do because it brings them joy to give and to stay in touch with a small group of close life-long friends. (Don't you wish your first boyfriend had been this cool?)

> *"My golden rule of networking is simple:*
> *Don't keep score."*
>
> —HARVEY MACKAY, AUTHOR OF *SWIM WITH THE SHARKS WITHOUT BEING EATEN ALIVE*

In the context of networking, you must recognize the power of the law of reciprocity and how it affects you and others. You have the choice whether to let it dictate your feelings and behavior, or to choose to create another experience for yourself. This leads me to another very cool idea.

The Pay It Forward Philosophy

The expression "pay it forward" is used to describe the concept of asking that a good turn be repaid, not to you directly, but to someone else in the future. It's the ultimate act of selfless kindness. It creates a endless cycle of good will.

Author Catherine Ryan Hyde wrote *Pay It Forward: A Novel*, which was later turned into a movie featuring actors Kevin Spacey and Helen Hunt. She suggests a unique response if someone does you a favor, something big, something you couldn't do on your own: Instead of paying it back, you pay it forward to three people, and the next day, each of them pay it forward to three more, and the day after, those twenty seven each pay it forward to another three. Eventually, that would come to more than 4.7 million people. With these kinds of numbers, the world would soon start to change—for the better!

My networking friend David has a similar idea and passion. He started a regional executive roundtable group. David is very active on LinkedIn and shares his leadership thoughts with executives who are going through the job search process. I first met David interviewing for a job at his company. I was overqualified for his marketing position and seeking more money than his budget allowed, so we didn't go forward with the employment relationship. Most people would walk away at this point, never contacting each other again. But there was some synergy between David and me and we stayed in touch during the next few years. David has called upon me to be a speaker at his Executive Roundtable events and to play an advisory role in his volunteer startup organization. He believes that every executive must adopt and practice a pay-it-forward philosophy. It's a leadership trait that creates positive energy, positive change, and positive relationships in the world.

These are the rules of the road in networking. Practice them and your journey will be more rewarding than ever before.

> *Practice giving of yourself with no strings attached.*
> *Whether it's your time, money, possessions, or*
> *knowledge, give without expectation of return.*

Next up is a frank discussion on your personal appearance and body language. If you don't pay attention to these little details, you could be inadvertently sending negative signals when you interact with others. First and last impressions count in networking (and in job interviews, business meetings, etc.) The good news is that fixing these problems is easier than you may think. So let's move on to assess what kind of impression you are leaving with your networking contacts, clients, and colleagues.

> *"Networking that matters is helping people achieve their goals."*
> — SETH GODIN, AUTHOR OF *PURPLE COW*

5. Road Grime and Door Dings

First and Last Impressions Count in Networking

How you present yourself when you network is very important. While I encourage you to be authentically you, I want you to present the best you possible. Everything matters, including how you look, how you act, your energy, and your attitude—and yes, what you drive. It all says something about you. It all communicates.

This section is dedicated to helping you become more aware of your visual communication so that you can make a conscious choice to improve it and get a better outcome when you network with other people.

Malcolm Gladwell, in his book *Blink: The Power of Thinking Without Thinking,* established a theory that our decision-making is influenced not only by careful study of all the facts and information, but also by an unconscious, split-second processing of a few particular details. As quickly as you can blink your eye, most of us draw conclusions about people, and Gladwell contends that these first impressions or gut instincts about things are pretty much on target.

Additional support comes from the study of Neuro Linguistic Programming (NLP), the science of how you run your brain. NLP is based upon the idea that everything we think, feel, and do is neurologically linked—every cell in our body is affected. The NLP Model of Communication suggests that we process external input through our senses and filter it through a variety of high-level individual filters. You can download an illustration of the NLP Model of Communication at ModernJedi.com/NLPmodel

This happens almost instantaneously, and we form an internal representation. We derive meaning from the external input, and that meaning shapes our thinking. That internal representation impacts your emotional state. It may make you feel happy, sad, silly, mad, annoyed, energized, etc. That particular emotional state triggers physiological responses. Your heart rate goes up or goes down, your breathing changes, you widen your eyes or narrow the glance, your face flushes, you clench your fists or cross your arms. All of this happens almost unconsciously. What comes next is your outward behavior. You do or say something. And that impacts your outcome.

If you want a better outcome, then change your behavior. How do you do that? You can start by changing how you think, how you feel, or what you do with your body. Make a small shift in any one of these, and the other two will follow. Neurological linkage at work; it's a beautiful design.

But it's not easy to control. Allan Pease, author of *The Definitive Book of Body Language,* asserts that "Our attitudes and emotions are continually revealed on our faces and we are completely unaware of it most of the time." We are so accustomed to doing what we do, without really thinking about it. We just respond; we react to what happens to us, and not always with the best outcome.

Body Language Intelligence

By increasing your skills of observation and paying more attention to your physiology and that of others, several wonderful things can happen for you:

- You suspend judgment of yourself and others long enough to create a better outcome.

- You gain additional sensory information that could help you decide the best course of action.

- You are less likely to overreact to situations or jump to incorrect conclusions.

- You become more self-aware and in control of your behavior.

- You are more fully present, which allows you to build and maintain rapport with other people.

I call this body language intelligence. It is an understanding and appreciation of your original mobile communication device—your body. It goes everywhere you go and is constantly sending messages to other people. In networking situations, your body language will have a large impact on your ability to make strong connections with people.

> *"Our attitudes and emotions are continually revealed on our faces and we are completely unaware of it most of the time."*
>
> —ALLAN PEASE, AUTHOR OF *THE DEFINITIVE BOOK OF BODY LANGUAGE*

Handshakes and Cell Phones

One of the first and last impressions that you make is with your handshake—the traditional greeting of hello and goodbye. The handshake serves to build trust between people as you bring someone into your personal space, press the flesh, and exchange energy. The handshake is a powerful nonverbal communication. Usually it goes fairly well, but then sometimes you miss or mess up.

Dan had invited me to speak at his upcoming training workshop. I was recommended to him by my good friend Julie. I was not being paid for this speaking "gig" and was doing it as a favor for Julie. Dan asked me to meet him at a local breakfast café to discuss the event. When I arrived, Dan was already at the table and was talking on his cell phone. I approached him and he gave me a head nod, signaling to me that he was just finishing up his call. I sat down. When his call was done, he shook my hand, giving me one of those fingertip, princess handshakes that I hate so much. His energy was wired; he was noticeably jittery and spoke very fast. Perhaps he had consumed too much caffeine? His eyes kept searching the room, as if he were expecting someone else. He kept his cell phone on the table, and when it inevitably went off, he answered it again during our networking meeting. Another interruption. Our meeting was rushed and awkward, and I was starting to regret having said yes to this speaking engagement.

What went wrong? Dan's body language told me so much more than his words could. In just a short 15 minutes, Dan had put distance between us and set the tone for our relationship. I don't think he was aware of that, and I don't think that was his intention. Dan failed to adjust his body language to meet the energy level of his guest. His cell phone behavior was perhaps the most offensive. I urge you to silence all mobile devices while networking or meeting with other people. The physiology of taking a call or looking at an incoming text during a meeting is all wrong.

Later on, I had the opportunity to share with Dan that I, like many professional women that I know, prefer a firmer handshake. "Treat me like your equal," I explained. He was surprised and told me that he shakes a woman's hand more gently out of respect for her. He learned this while growing up in his family. One of his female co-workers was in the room during this discussion, and she chimed in to agree with me. She said that she hated when men do that to her. This was a teaching moment for both of us. Dan got important feedback on how his handshake was received by women (at least two of us), and I learned more about Dan's background and intention. He wasn't such a rude guy after all; he just had limited exposure to professional businesswomen. We practiced shaking hands until he got it just the way I liked it. I walked away with an improved impression of Dan. I hope he felt better about me too.

There are three qualities of a professional handshake:

1. **Complete:** You want to make full contact, that is web-to-web, with the groove between your index finger and your thumb coming together with the other person's, without any gaps in that space.

2. **Equal:** Make sure both people's palms are in vertical position. Neither party should attempt to dominate or be submissive, which is communicated unconsciously when one hand is underneath or on top of the other person's palm. There should be no bending at the wrist.

3. **Receptive:** Apply the same pressure that you receive. You don't want to hurt someone with too much pressure. "Bone crushers" and "vice grips" should be avoided at all times. Your handshake should be smooth and easy. It should never feel or look abrasive, nor have abrupt or jerky motions. At the other extreme, you don't want to give them a wimpy grip. Think about "hugging the hand" by wrapping your fingers around their palm. Beware of your index finger extending up and on to the inside of their wrist. This sends the signal that you are dominating, by taking more control of their body. Remember that the handshake exchange should feel good to both parties. It should never create physical pain or displeasure, or send mixed signals.

A few other enhancing tips to make your handshake a positive experience include: smile when you shake hands, look them in the eye, and introduce yourself. Repeat their name (e.g., "Nice to meet you, Gary Smith.") so that you begin to lock their name into your short term memory. Give it three to five pumps and then let go of their hand. Hanging on to their hand and continuous up and down motion becomes awkward quickly, if not a bit creepy.

One last comment about handshakes. While we live in a global economy, different nations have their own dos and don'ts with regard to nonverbal communication. Before you travel abroad for business or pleasure, I recommend that you read up on the social etiquette norms for that country. Be sure your body language, including your handshake, is appropriate and acceptable. Your flexibility and globally savvy will go a long way to enhancing international relations and your career and business success.

Power Up Your Professional Image

A big part of your visual impact is how you dress, how you groom yourself—your physical appearance. Many people I know are very self-conscious about their weight, yet they ignore other important aspects of their appearance. It's not just about your body size and shape; it's what you do with it. Fat, thin, young, old, tall, short—whatever configuration your body is, you can learn to leverage it to your advantage. You must pay attention to the details, and take steps to make the necessary enhancements.

No one likes to hear the complaints of a thin person, but let me share mine with you. Clothes hang off me. Nothing fits well. Hem lines from slacks that I buy in the store are always too long. The new waist lines drop lower on my hips, and I am uncomfortable with that look and fit. It gives me the appearance of having droopy drawers or that teen look that I have certainly outgrown. I hate high-heeled shoes as they are dreadfully uncomfortable (and dangerous) for me. I have a closet full of clothes and shoes that don't really work for me, and I am not alone. The majority of American women have the same problem. We wear only 20 percent of what's in our closet, but we keep buying, buying, buying. Is it a problem of retail therapy or a desperate attempt to find something that fits and looks good?

In 2009, I had the good fortune of meeting and networking with a woman named Janice, who is an unusual combination of financial planner and makeup artist. She has a side business with Mary Kay Cosmetics as an independent beauty consultant.

Despite having worked for Maybelline cosmetics for three years, I'm really not that much into makeup. But Janice struck me as an interesting person, a motivated woman—certainly worth getting together with for coffee. Deep down, I was worried that she would ask me to host a Mary Kay home party—something I really didn't want to do. I was thinking of all the other ways in which I might be able to help her without having to host a party.

As a result of our first networking coffee, we collaborated on a series of events called "Power Up Your Professional Image," focused on helping career-minded women get an edge in the workplace. We have invited many service professionals to assist with this program including image consultants, wardrobe specialists, skin care and color cosmetic consultants, photographers, communication specialists, life coaches, even financial advisors. And the day is filled with networking opportunities, in a safe, supportive, and invigorating environment.

As a result of being involved with this group, I realized that I needed to invest in my own professional image. I hired an image consultant to do a color analysis and a closet audit to determine what worked and what didn't. We weeded through my closet and donated about half of my wardrobe. It was a great investment of time and money. I then hired a tailor specializing in alterations for professional women to custom alter my core remaining pieces, including suits, slacks, blouses and even sweaters. If it didn't fit, it didn't stay, including shoes. I re-examined my purchasing strategies and wardrobe priorities. I now value quality of clothing above quantity, and am more committed to buying things that look good, fit well, and last. Trendy fashion clothing that creates an instant retail thrill for me is out of style forevermore.

There is magic in networking;
you just need to be open to it.

In addition to this change in buying pattern, the "Power Up" initiative has led me to meet many connected women. I have gained valuable new insight, knowledge, and opportunities. All of this value was created from one networking meeting over coffee. Yes, there is magic in networking; you just need to be open to it.

Attention to Detail

This part is perhaps the hardest for me to write, because I don't always practice what I preach in regard to keeping a clean car. People make instant judgments about you based upon what you drive. Consider it automotive grooming, but an occasional car wash can go a long way in improving your professional image and sending the right signals to other people. Here's one time that I realized how important that was.

At a regional conference I met Jack Mitchell, the author of two books, *Hug Your Customers* and *Hug Your People*, and the CEO of the very successful high-end men and women's clothier Mitchells/Richards in Connecticut. Jack was the keynote speaker at the conference. (Hint: Always introduce yourself to the speaker and follow up. Speakers are usually very connected and interesting people.)

I reached out to Jack after the meeting. I also met his terrific executive assistant. He invited me down to his store in Westport, Connecticut, to discuss ideas and a possible collaboration. It was rather intimidating to think about what I was going to wear to this meeting. Jack's shoes probably cost more than my entire outfit, including jewelry and wedding ring! But I had the impression that Jack was a kind and down-to-earth person and that he would receive me well.

The meeting went well until the moment where Jack graciously offered to give me a box of his book *Hug Your Customers* and said that he'd bring them out to my car personally. This was a very gentlemanly thing to do. However, it sent me into a near internal panic as I could see in my mind's eye how filthy and unkempt my car was. I would have to open the trunk for him. What was in there? How dirty was my green car? Could you even tell it was the color green? What was strewn in the backseat that he might see? My briefcase, papers, clothing, hangers, maybe even dry cleaner plastic bags? This was going to be a killer last impression. I was sweating now. There was no wiggling out of this one.

In the end, I survived this professional image violation. Jack went on to hire me for a short engagement. If I could do it all over again, I might have taken 30 extra minutes to have my car washed. I would have cleaned out my stuff and made my vehicle a little more respectable— just in case.

Olfactory Offenses

How good do you smell? Do you smoke? Do you wear a lot of perfume or use heavily scented deodorant? Do you douse yourself in fragrant essential oils? Do you have coffee breath much of the time? All of these scents create strong first and lasting impressions, and most of the time they are negative. If you are a smoker, you need to be aware that the smell of cigarette smoke permeates your hair, clothing, car, and anything you touch. It's like the cloud that followed Pig-Pen, the character from the Charles Schulz "Peanuts" cartoon.

Your particular habit and lifestyle choice may have a significant negative impact on your professional image, and most people won't tell you what they are thinking. Before you send me hate mail or put this book in the trash out of anger, please remember my intention is to help you be more professionally successful with networking and relationship building. I also want you to live a full, healthy, and rich life. Smoking is counterproductive to these goals.

> *Attention to detail is what turns good into great, average into exceptional, and common into extraordinary. I want that to be your reputation.*

For other bad smells, you need to take proactive action. Carry a toothbrush in your purse (carefully sealed of course); eat breath mints before meeting with people; rinse out your mouth with water more frequently (a suggestion from my dentist); and pass up the perfume and go natural. (This is especially important when traveling on airplanes or attending conferences. Some people are highly allergic to perfumes.)

If you are meeting with people after a meal, you might want to watch how much garlic you eat. While excellent for your blood and health and absolutely delicious in my opinion, garlic will permeate your pores and you will smell of it. This might irritate other people who don't enjoy garlic or didn't partake of it that day. On the other hand, garlic will keep the networking vampires at a safe distance. These folks can suck the living daylights out of your professional network.

Attention to detail is what turns good into great, average into exceptional, and common into extraordinary. I want that to be your reputation. I want you to be known as a professional who is well put together, has a high level of self-awareness and self-control, and can conduct themselves with grace and decorum in any environment. Make no mistake, this level of mastery takes work. It requires you to pay attention to the details of how you show up.

Next stop we'll discuss how networking can help you better manage your career. Proactive networking allows you to move confidently and navigate the inevitable ups and downs of the job market.

> *"There are four ways, and only four ways, in which we have contact with the world. We are evaluated and classified by these four contacts: what we do, how we look, what we say, and how we say it."*
> — DALE CARNEGIE (188-1955), AUTHOR OF *HOW TO WIN FRIENDS AND INFLUENCE PEOPLE*

6. A Fork in the Road

Networking through Career Changes

Very few people know exactly where they are headed, have everything completely planned out in advance, and arrive exactly where they want to be when they want to be there. There are just too many unknowns—too many bumps in the road. It's called life.

As you think about your career and where it might lead, you need to build a little flexibility into your overall "plan." With the increased frequency of change, such as disruptive technologies that impact entire industries, companies that go out of business or have to reduce their workforces just to stay afloat, you'll need to not only keep your skills up, but also to keep your network alive and healthy.

Many people resort to networking only after they get laid off, fired, downsized, made redundant, or quit out of frustration. That's like coming to a fork in the road that you hadn't anticipated and sitting there for a long time trying to decide how you got there and which road you should take next. If you are on the freeway, with other cars whizzing by you, you don't have the luxury of time to think through that decision. As a result, you may go in a direction that takes you off course.

Wouldn't it be better to have anticipated that fork in the road? Do some contingency planning in advance, so if it should happen, you will be able to respond more quickly and confidently. Remember that networking is the art of building and maintaining mutually beneficial relationships *before you need them.*

Networking While You Have a Job

The best time to be networking is while you are gainfully employed and doing well. This is when you may think you need it the least, but actually you are in the best position to leverage it. By making the time to network while you have a job, you are building alliances and keeping your lifelines alive. New and better opportunities may be presented to you unexpectedly, or you can put feelers out there and attract them to you.

Many people I know feel they have to be covert about networking while they are employed by others. This mindset is more transactional— that is, I'm looking for a better job. Posting your resume on Indeed is not what I call networking. That's job hunting. Networking is about relationships with individuals, not just companies or open positions.

The other reason that you are in the best position to network while you have a job is that you are in a good position to help others. You may be short on time, but you are rich in resources and internal connections. People don't forget you when you've helped them.

What can you do specifically to keep your network alive and growing while you have a job? It's important that you actively participate on social media. The following steps are easy to implement even if you are super busy:

- Get yourself a LinkedIn account and complete your profile with a professional photograph, so people can easily identify you.

- Invite people you already know to "link in" with you.

- At least once a week, share a relevant update, photo, or article that's tied to your area of expertise. This gives you additional visibility and adds value to the people in your network.

> *"Network continually—85 percent of all jobs are filled through contacts and personal references."*
> —BRIAN TRACY, AUTHOR OF *CHANGE YOUR THINKING CHANGE YOUR LIFE*

If your current employer frowns on the use of work hours for social media, then make time for it after work. It is an important part of maintaining your personal brand and keeping your network alive. Remember, network or not work.

For more ideas on how to use social media to your networking advantage, read Chapter 17 "Mind the Gap."

Beyond the Cubicle: Networking Outside of Work

Think about how often you actually "leave the building" to meet with people who work for someone else. If you are in sales, you have many client-facing opportunities. But I am talking about connecting with people who are not directly related to your job function or company goals.

Making time to build relationships outside your work world is like diversifying your financial portfolio. It's a smart investment strategy. The mix of people whom you know is important because it balances your overall risk. When one thing is down, the other investments buoy the overall portfolio performance.

Dan Schawbel author, of *Me 2.0: 4 Steps to Building Your Future*, suggests that career professionals take an active role in networking outside of their place of employment. He advises us "to secure your brand, spend more of your time networking outside of your company than within."

My advice is that you don't allow yourself to get tunnel vision and think that you are safe and happy connecting with only the people in your immediate work world. That office illusion may self-implode at any moment. You must have lifelines established outside your four walls of employment.

In-Between Floors: Networking at Work

You can also network inside your current company. This means you must reach out to people who are in different departments, different divisions, and different disciplines. To build these strong relationships, I urge you to get to know people beyond just their role on the project or for the company. Talk about other things that are important in their lives, not just the job or quarterly performance.

Make it a point to have lunch with different people in your organization each week. This is a perfect time to spread your reach and make new friends across the company. You can even do this if you are a part-time employee, contractor, or vendor.

Meet Kathleen: the woman who experienced twelve minute unemployment. Kathleen was working as a contractor with a major insurance company. She got paid through an employment agency, but Kathleen took a proactive approach to both managing her work and building relationships across her client's company. She felt as though it was her company.

Suddenly, the director of her assigned project called to let her know that the project was taking a different direction, and her contract assignment was going to be cut short. He encouraged her to reach out to others in the company to see if she could secure a new assignment. Kathleen shared with me that after that phone call she endured a two-minute state of panic.

{ *Making time to build relationships outside your work world is like diversifying your financial portfolio. It's a smart investment strategy.* }

Learning that you are going to lose your job can do a number on your head. She quickly pulled herself together and got on the phone to connect with many of the people in the organization with whom she had built friendly relationships. After the third phone call, she connected with another director who told her that he could place her on an assignment, to fill the role of a woman who was leaving on maternity. She had verbally secured a new position for herself within 12 minutes! This would not have been possible for Kathleen if she did not have excellent networking and people skills and established relationships in place. As a contractor, she could have been viewed as an "outsider," but she was savvy enough to have built up many positive connections on the inside. This paid off for her very quickly in her hour of need.

Staying Motivated During Your Job Search

It's difficult to stay motivated during a job search. Days turn into weeks, weeks into months, and soon you find yourself falling into a mini-depression. During the economic meltdown of 2008 and the years that followed, there were high levels of unemployment. Even after the economy started to pick up, companies were reluctant to hire. They kept hold of their cash, as millions of highly skilled professionals found themselves facing long periods of unemployment—some lasting for 10 to 18 month stretches. It's a miserable experience indeed.

Networking is a must-do activity for any job search, but there are things you need to remember to keep yourself in the most positive state of mind and body while you network and look for that next great job. Here are a few suggestions from my keynote, "Motivated Job Search."

BE MINDFUL

Cheryl Jones is a mindfulness and well-being speaker, coach, and author. She recommends job seekers practice mindfulness throughout the search process. She asks you to imagine that the space between this job and the next is fertile ground for what is yet to come. Imagine that you are in preparation mode, even though you don't know what you are preparing for. Ultimately you must protect your best asset, which is your health. You must remember to take care of yourself during this process, so that you can present yourself as a strong, vital person inside and out. Exercise and better nutrition may be just the ticket you need to purchase when you are in between jobs.

BE VALUED

You must always remember that you are significant, despite your present circumstance or shortcomings. People are not attracted to those who appear to be weak, bitter, or lost. To increase your networking success during your job search process, you must strengthen your inner core. No matter what your current circumstances are, you must continue to believe in yourself. You must envision a positive future for you and others. If you don't value yourself, it will be difficult for others to value you. You want their support, not their sympathy.

BE POSITIVELY RESILIENT

When you lose your job, it feels like you've been knocked down. In fact, the job search process can feel like one big boxing match in which you are getting repeatedly knocked down (or ignored, which is worse). I'm going to suggest that you become more like Andy Warhol, the famous American artist. In October 1956, Warhol received a rejection letter from the Museum of Modern Art of New York, refusing his offer to donate his artwork, "Shoe." Mr. Warhol kept this rejection letter in his files, but didn't keep it in his heart. He went on to build a successful career and legacy. By being positively resilient, you too can be like Andy Warhol: committed, confident, and able to put yourself out there over and over again until you realize your greatness.

BE CONNECTED

This is synonymous with networking. Having strong relationships and staying actively engaged with people will help keep you positively motivated throughout your job search. In fact, many people develop their understanding and passion for networking during a job search process. You come to realize how fabulous it is to give and receive help from others. It is beyond me why on earth anyone would abandon this powerful, positive habit once they are re-employed.

BE VISIBLE AND MOBILE

This next pointer on networking for job search success comes from Claudia Lindsey, a marketing executive who found herself out of work and needing to network to land her next opportunity. She recommends that you manage your personal visibility and mobility by accumulating connections who are motivated to share information, ideas, and opportunities. These valuable connections are most likely to be outside your close circles. They have access to different information pools than you do. If they have a positive impression of you, they will be more likely to help you. Claudia recommends that job seekers accumulate more "distant" connections who are motivated to share information, and to actively follow up with them.

> *To increase your networking success during the job search process, you must strengthen your inner core. You must believe in yourself.*

BE APPRECIATIVE

Finally, expressing your appreciation is paramount for your success in the job search process, in networking, and in life in general. Being appreciative is an active, conscious effort to acknowledge and thank people for the good things they have brought into your world. Don't assume they know how you feel about them. Tell them directly. Saying "thank you" is one of the most powerful leadership habits you can practice. To show my appreciation in networking, I like to use these tips and tricks:

- I send *Say It Forward* mini cards with inspiring quotes that are crowd-sourced. This company was founded by my friend

Sandra Centorino and her two daughters. Check it out at sayitinternational.com

- I insert gift cards to Dunkin' Donuts, Starbucks, Panera Bread or Subway with my thank you cards. My friend Mark Shepard likes to refer to this as "bucks of love."

- Create and send a custom greeting card with pictures and positive messages using SendOutCards, an online greeting card and gifting system. They also offer motivating card inserts that you can tuck in to the greeting card to make it just a little more special for the recipient. If you want to create a super show of appreciation, you can send the two-pack Kosher brownies along with your greeting card. I've never met anyone who didn't love getting that in the mail. Try it out and send your first card for free: www.MotivatingCards.com (p.s. you'll have to pay for the brownies if you want to include them with your free first card mailing.)

You can show your appreciation in many different ways, but I believe the most powerful way is to say it verbally. I remember a story that a former colleague of mine, Brian O'Grady, told me of his boss, Mike Hiskett. They were both in sales, one reporting to the other. At the end of every phone call, Mike, the sales VP, would say to Brian, the sales manager, "Thank you for all you do for me and this company. I appreciate it." How many sales leaders do you know who are known for that? You are more likely to hear the phrase, "What have you done for me lately?" This conscious habit to express appreciation earned Mike a top place in Brian's mind and heart. They will be connected for a very long time—long after either one or both of them leave the employment of that particular company. Appreciation bonds people together in positive, permanent ways. Expressing your appreciation will bring you joy, energy, and motivation to carry on.

Be a Responsible Driver of Your Career

Clearly, networking is a must-have strategy for any professional in an active job search. But it is also a savvy strategy for people who are serious about managing their careers. Gone are the days when the company takes full responsibility for your career path and development. It's in your hands now. This passing of the baton is not only appropriate, but it is empowering. Yet, many people find themselves neglecting their networks once they become gainfully employed. They abandon their network and dedicate all their time, energy, and attention on their day job. As a result, their network dries up. What happens when you need to jump start it? That's the focus of our next chapter.

> *"If you're not networking, you're not working."*
> — DENIS WAITLEY, AUTHOR OF *THE PSYCHOLOGY OF WINNING*

7. Jump Start

Re-engage Your Network after a
Long Period of Neglect

Have you ever gone on vacation only to come home and find that your car won't start? This could be a reflection that cars left unattended for long periods of time go battery-dead and need a jump to get going again. Smart drivers always carry jumper cables in their car. But the idea of having to attach those cables to the battery can be intimidating. Is it the red cable to the positive charge or the black cable? No one likes the big shock.

So what can you do to avoid this emergency situation? I suggest that you keep your car going.

Now imagine this same situation but in the context of networking. You have been away from your car (your professional network, in this case) for a long period of time. Perhaps you were on a special work assignment that demanded huge hours, or you moved out of the area and went back to school, immersing yourself in a whole new world. Whatever reason took you away, you have not been in touch with the people in your professional network for years.

Now something happens, and you need them again. You lost your job; you were laid off; you were fired; or you got divorced. The world as you knew it suddenly changed—and not necessarily for the better. Now you realize that you need to start networking again. It can be a very awkward feeling to have to pick up the phone and call people whom you haven't spoken to in quite some time. It feels like a cold call, but worse. What do you say? How do you start the conversation? What will they think of you? Will they be there for you again?

I have received several of these phone calls in my life. I have even had to make a few in my day. Here's a story of one such experience.

I worked for a company whose chief marketing officer was let go. The CEO asked my colleague Jim and me to step up to the plate and co-manage the marketing department of 100 people while they searched for a replacement. I was hoping that I could prove myself in this interim role and might be considered for the position. No such luck. So Jim and I spent many hours together, coordinating, communicating, and brainstorming. We got to know each other pretty well. I liked him.

Then I was let go from the company. It was a blessing in disguise, but at the time, the dismissal was a big sting. The day I left, most of my colleagues came to wish me well and promised to stay in touch and help me in any way that they could, including Jim.

After a few weeks of licking my wounds, I jumped back in the saddle and began the job search process. I called Jim to see if he had any ideas or connections that could help me. No return phone call. I knew he was busy and had his hands full, so I continued with my outreach efforts to others. I called him again and left another voice mail. No call back. At this time, I was beginning to think that our closeness was an illusion or relationship of convenience. It's odd how when you leave a company, former colleagues often treat you as if you have a deadly contagious disease. Those who remain at the company act as if they have been instructed not to be in touch with those that have left the company. An unwritten policy?

Two years later, I received word from a former colleague and friend that there was another round of layoffs at the company. Jim had been let go along with a horde of other people. Two weeks later, I got a phone call from Jim asking me if I could help him in his job search. It was an awkward call for both of us. There were all sorts of thoughts going on inside my head. Does he really care about me, or is he just using me? Is he a reluctant networker, introvert, or person who just doesn't know how to build and maintain relationships outside the company?

Of course, I helped Jim as best I could, but I didn't go out of my way. He has since landed another job, and life is back to normal for him. I haven't heard from him since. The battery charge of our relationship has gone cold once again. We have both abandoned it. I suspect that this experience is more the norm than the exception. Many people view networking as job search activity only. For many, networking is an event, a tactic, and an unpleasant one at that. That kind of thinking is very short-sighted.

But what if you had a different attitude about it? What if you treated networking as strategy for life? What if relationship building was more of a philosophy for you and that you valued people and relationships even more highly than you did projects and promotions? What if your professional network was always there for you, ready to help you, assist you, to support you in the good times and the bad times? What if you never had to make an awkward call like Jim had to?

> *People don't know what's going on in your life unless you tell them. The act of communicating will help you maintain your relationships through time.*

Keep Your Battery Charged

The best way that I know to maintain a robust and active professional network is to run it continually. Never let it go cold. Never abandon it for long periods of time. If you are going to be tied up for a while with an intense project, let your network know what you are taking on. Let them know that you may be out of touch for a while, but that you'll re-emerge after a certain period.

Robyn Greenspan does this well. Robyn was the editor-in-chief for ExecuNet.com, the world's largest online network for executive level leaders. Robyn's job was to lead a team and provide intelligent and timely content, professional development, and networking opportunities for business leaders to help them better manage their companies and their careers. I learned from Robyn's boss, Dave Opton, the founder and CEO of ExecuNet.com, that Robyn was in "writer's jail"—sequestered behind closed doors for the next six weeks until her annual report was completed. She put a humorous sign on her door to let her colleagues know that she would be heads-down for that period of time. I caught wind of this through Dave and asked him to take a photo of the sign on her door and e-mail it to me.

He did, and I immediately turned that photo into a customized greeting card and sent her a note of encouragement. That single act of kindness has taken our relationship to the next level.

The point of this story is that people don't know what's going on in your life unless you tell them. If you tell them, they can support you, understand you, and give you what you need (even if that is to leave you alone for a period of time while you concentrate on something big). Do what Robyn did so well and communicate with those around you. With the social media tools now available, we can cast this message out to more people in our professional and personal networks. The act of communication will help to maintain your relationships through time. You'll never need a jumpstart again.

> *"More business is lost every year through neglect than through any other cause."*
> —ROSE KENNEDY (1890-1995), MOTHER OF
> PRESIDENT JOHN F. KENNEDY

Checklist #1

Good work. You are on your way. You've completed Part I of your networking journey. Part II will introduce you to several important techniques that will enhance your networking skill and confidence. When you've completed these affirmations and actions, you will be ready for Part II.

☐ I am prepared to push myself out of my comfort zone to meet new people and build new professional relationships.

☐ I am willing to spend the necessary time, money, and energy to get more organized and disciplined about networking so that I can effectively incorporate it into my daily routine.

☐ I've completed the My World Exercise (download at americasmarketingmotivator.com/my-world/) and know who is in my current network by name.

☐ I understand who is in my Top 50 contact list. I'm prepared to invest more in these relationships with a greater frequency of touch and higher quality of communication.

☐ I have practiced and gotten external feedback on my handshake. It is neither too soft nor too hard, but achieves the three qualities of a professional handshake: complete, equal, and receptive.

PART II

Start Driving
Effective Networking Techniques

8. Go the Same Speed

How to Build Rapid Rapport When Networking

Imagine that you are on the highway, and you're racing along, passing all the cars one by one. You are on a mission, determined to get where you are going, or perhaps you are enjoying yourself, and the speed takes on a life of its own. Whatever the motivation, you are passing a lot of people, until you see those flashing lights in your rear view mirror. Busted.

I remember once when this happened to me in Massachusetts. I was late for a coaching session with a client in Boston. I had to make up some time, so my driving was more "pedal to the metal" than normal. I became obsessed with getting away from a very large truck that was on the road, fearing it might accidentally throw windshield-breaking rocks my way. The police officer didn't say much; in fact, he didn't show me much attention or respect at all. He just wrote me that $210 ticket and left me there talking to myself. He wasn't in the mood to listen to a bunch of excuses, nor was he interested in building rapport and getting to know me, another out-of-state speeder in his book. He was just doing his job.

When I shared this news with my husband, he reminded me of two important things. First, the car does have cruise control, and this would help me keep a constant speed on the open highway. Cruise control also improves gas mileage and efficiency and is less demanding physically on the driver. Second, he also shared a sensible strategy with me: If you can help it, try not to be out in front of the other cars by any great distance. Keep with the pack. This way you are protected. A police officer would have to pull over all the cars in your cluster, and this would be difficult to do.

Speeding Tickets Are Also Given in Networking

Speeding is also an issue in networking. When you talk too fast or move too fast when networking with a person of a different style and speed, you push that individual away without even knowing it or intending it. Visually dominant people tend to be fast talkers. They often don't even finish their sentences because they are moving on to another topic. They see in pictures, sometimes movies. They are rapid processors of information.

Now imagine what happens when a visually dominant person meets with a more relaxed, more methodical kinesthetically dominant person. These folks like to be comfortable, they feel things, they reflect, they speak more slowly. When you mix a visual person with a kinesthetic person, you can often get a painful mismatch of styles unless one or both of you know how to be flexible and how to pace to lead.

Pace to Lead

This is a simple and powerful concept that you can learn and apply in almost any business or personal situation. It doesn't require any fancy training, just a high level of awareness of what's going on in the moment. If you want to connect and build rapport with someone, then you need to let him or her set the pace and lead for the first few minutes. You want to observe that person's body language and vocal pacing and then match it. If the individual is sitting back in a chair in a relaxed fashion and speaking quietly and slowly, you want to start off this way as well. Make a conscious effort to be at his or her speed, even if you are excited, enthusiastic, and pumped up with caffeine. Purposely slow down and follow the other person's lead.

> *If you want to connect and build rapport with someone, then you need to let him or her set the pace and lead for the first few minutes.*

The beautiful thing about building rapport with others is that the connection is made largely at an unconscious level. You feel good about others and are comfortable with them. Sometimes you get the feeling that you've met them before. You are starting to like them, and likability is a key factor in business and professional success. You have created a foundation from which the conversation can flow and a relationship can develop. This is a solid base from which trust can begin to develop through time.

In a matter of moments, you can build rapid rapport with others. Soon they will begin to follow your lead. You will know that you have rapport with them when you begin to lead and move into your natural speed and style and they follow.

Mismatching Body Language and Energy Levels

I met Jack through my local chamber of commerce. He heard me speak at a seminar at our local library that offers a fantastic series of business programs. Jack called and invited me to meet him for coffee to discuss some business opportunities he was developing. He indicated that he might want to hire me as a marketing consultant. I was excited to hear more as Jack might become a new (paying) client. When Jack and I sat down for coffee, I quickly became engaged and eager to learn more. My brain went into full brainstorming mode. My mouth quickly followed, spurting out all sorts of ideas. Jack sat back in his chair and I assumed he was taking in all of this incredible free marketing advice. I came up with one brilliant suggestion that he immediately applied that afternoon with a new prospect and landed a new piece of business. Jack shared this success with me. I knew at that moment that I had the consulting assignment in the bag. I had just demonstrated my value.

Surprisingly, Jack selected the other marketing consultant, not me. When I asked him why, he said that he felt that the other guy was a better fit for him and his business needs. I was shocked and stunned. How much more did he need to see? Clearly I could help him accelerate his business. The truth was that Jack didn't need more, he needed less from me. During my networking meeting with him, I completely misread his body language signals, ignored important verbal clues, and unconsciously went into hyper-Kathy mode. I was fast-talking, overpowering with my energy, and overly demonstrative. I was more than Jack could handle. I failed to build rapport with Jack in a way that he was comfortable with. I exhausted him.

Has that ever happened to you? If so, consider what outcome might have been possible if you had exercised a little more awareness and self-control. It doesn't take much effort to adjust your energy level in the initial moments of the conversation so that the other person is more comfortable with you. Mirroring and matching techniques and rapport building skills can work to get you better service in restaurants, banks, and retail stores. It also works effectively on the phone.

It's More than Just Words that Count

When you are face-to-face with people, 38% of the meaning they take away from your communication is influenced by "paralinguistic" factors or your tone of voice, according to UCLA Professor Albert Mehrabian. His well-renowned and often-quoted study conducted in the 1970's is referred to as the "7%-38%-55% Rule." This means your communication in face-to-face situations is influenced by:

- 7% verbal: the actual words that are spoken;

- 38% vocal: the way the words are said (tone of voice) and;

- 55% visual: what the listener sees you do when you speak, including your visual appearance, your facial expressions, and your body language.

This theory is useful in explaining the importance of meaning, as distinct from words. Understanding the difference between words and meaning is a vital capability for effective communications and relationships. And it starts in those first few minutes of getting to know someone.

Leverage Your Voice

Consider how much more influence you could have if you worked on your voice. According to Dr. Mehrabian, it's the second biggest lever you have in communication, some 38%. Some people are unaware how unpleasant their voice sounds to others. Think of how often you get that visceral reaction when you listen to someone who speaks in a raspy, nasal, tense, breathy, high-pitched, and otherwise annoying voice. It creates a negative impression, and unconsciously distances people, rather than drawing them closer.

Why does the quality of your voice matter? Consider the words of Arthur Samuel Joseph, founder of The Vocal Awareness Institute, and author of several books including one of my favorites, *Vocal Leadership*, "You make your living through your voice. Your mouth is not just your mind out loud." The quality of your voice communicates a great deal about you to others. It's reflects what kind of leader you are. Being consciously aware not only of what you are saying, but how you are saying it, will give you more vocal power, more confidence, and more credibility.

What can be done to improve your voice? There are many things you can do, such as working with a vocal coach, doing daily vocal exercises, and warming up your voice before meetings and presentations. To improve my own voice, I have been studying and practicing vocal awareness for the last few years. Quite frankly, it has been life changing. It has helped me to grow professionally, and it has made a material difference in my business growth and career. This work is a commitment to mastery and to vocal leadership. I have discovered that only a select group of professionals is willing to do this level of work.

To help the rest, I came up with a simple concept called the vocal dashboard. It is a very cool and powerful instrument panel that makes you more aware and gives you more variety and control when you speak. It can make your voice more interesting to listen to. We all have access to our vocal dashboards, but most of us set it and forget it, never adjusting the dials to leverage the power that our voices truly possess.

Rather than just talking, consider playing with the knobs on your vocal dashboard to power up your communication. Developing greater mastery over your voice is not just a skill reserved for singers, actors, and professional speakers. It is for anyone who wants to be heard, has something to say, and could use a little more influence in his or her life.

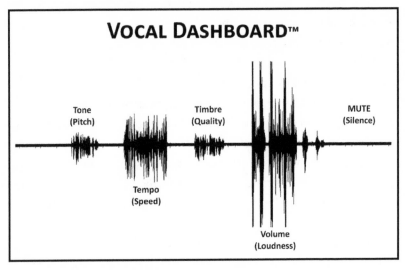

Let's examine the five basic dials on your vocal dashboard:

1. Tone of your voice (pitch)
2. Tempo of your voice (speed)
3. Timbre of your voice (quality)
4. Volume of your voice (loudness)
5. Mute (the powerful sound of silence)

Expand Your Tonal Range

Think of a professionally trained singer, one who can hit high notes and low notes. Now think of someone you know who has an annoyingly high-pitched voice and never wavers from it. Now think of what you sound like when you are giving a command to your dog, and you really want the little darling to listen to you. You probably lower your voice and use an authoritative and commanding voice. These are all examples of tone or pitch. We all have a range. The goal is to use the full range of our tone, and select the pitch that will work best for the particular outcome we desire at that moment.

The Good and Bad of Upspeak

Upspeak is what happens when a person makes a question out of a sentence that isn't a question. It is the result of lifting your tone or pitch of your voice at the wrong time (usually at the end of the sentence). Upspeak is a common affliction for teenagers, most women, and many younger professionals. Upspeak can put doubt in the listener's mind and can cause that person to think that you don't know what you are talking about. If you are overusing the upspeak vocal pattern, you may be negatively chipping away at your professional credibility.

Jack Griffith, author of *How to Say It at Work*, suggests that we avoid ending declarative sentences in a rising note. This is a verbal bad habit more common to women than men. It makes a statement sound tentative, even doubtful, as if the speaker were seeking approval.

To better understand what upspeak sounds like, watch the short television interview with me and Steve Adubato on my YouTube Channel or search under the key phrase "Body Language and Vocal Power."

You can use upspeak strategically to your advantage. There will be times when you want to introduce doubt in people's minds. For example, you might say, "Is this solution good enough?" (Lifting your voice on the word "enough.") Or even use it with a statement such as, "This is the best we can do." (Lifting the voice on the words "best" or "do.")

You can also leverage upspeak to gain agreement from people if you accompany it with a positive head nod. For example: "You like this?" (Nodding the head and lifting the voice on the word "this.") This technique is one that you'd have to practice a great deal. There is sales power when you can get the prospect's head bobbing.

Tempo: The Metronome of Your Speech

You may not realize it, but you have control over how quickly or how slowly you speak. You'll want to be careful not to talk too fast with someone who has a slower pace of speech. If you desire to build rapport with this person, you must step out of your normal speech pattern and purposefully slow down your communication. When you get practiced at this, you'll discover that you can apply this powerful technique to many different situations, including those outside of networking. For example, if you are giving a public speech or presentation, you'll want to slow down your normal conversational pace by 20 percent. You can also make yourself a more interesting speaker by varying the tempo of your delivery throughout your presentation, speeding up and slowing down among different thoughts and ideas. This variation in tempo can serve to hold your audience's attention. Remember that monotone voices can put audiences to sleep almost as fast as too many boring PowerPoint slides.

Probably the bigger challenge is for a normally slow talker to speed it up in order to build rapport with someone new. This can be physically tiring for them. However, the duration that you need to sustain this unusual activity will be brief, perhaps two to three minutes. Once you have established rapport, you can use your body language and your vocal patterns to slow down and open up the other person and bring the conversation to a place where you are more comfortable. This is the art of pacing to lead. If you do it well, you eventually get to lead.

> *If you are giving a public speech or presentation, you'll want to slow down your normal conversational pace by 20 percent.*

Quality May Vary

You don't have to have a beautiful singing voice in order to be effective in leveraging it to build relationships. Quality or timbre (rhymes with amber), as it is referred to vocally, has many different aspects to it. The goal is to develop a full and rich speaking voice that is known as forward resonance. You can also strive to be clear as a bell and enunciate every consonant in every word, creating a formal speech sound effect. While this creates the impression of being articulate and perhaps highly educated, you may unconsciously be pushing certain people away from you. If this sounds like you, here's what you can do that maintains your high standards, but utilizes flexibility for the sake of building rapport with others. Try adding more texture to your voice. Think of when you have a head cold or a stuffy nose. You get that radio voice that other people find sexy and attractive. Sometimes a raspy quality to the voice makes it stand out and makes it somewhat endearing. You can learn to adjust the timbre of your voice in certain situations while still maintaining your authenticity and personal values. Be careful not to make your change in timbre too obvious or extreme. You don't want to come off as a bad actor. Practice on the phone, matching the texture of the caller's voice.

Please Don't Clear Your Throat

In my work as an executive presentation coach and trainer, I have become keenly aware of how the sound of one's voice impacts the message and the perception of one's leadership presence. Clearing your throat repeatedly during a networking meeting, a phone call, a presentation, or a job interview can alienate your audience and cause them to doubt your expertise. There are many reasons why we clear our throats. For example, medical conditions, seasonal allergies, emotional variables, or habitual response to stress can cause us to feel the need to clear our throats. But it turns out that clearing your throat is counterproductive. According to Arthur Samuel Joseph "clearing the throat badly irritates the vocal mechanism, wearing it down much like grinding gears in your car. To function effectively, the vocal folds need air. Throat clearing causes the vocal folds to rub together without air…and therefore hurts the voice." It can end up sounding like that dreadful noise made when someone grinds the gears of an automobile with a manual transmission.

Clearing your throat during a phone interview can also send a red flag to the hiring manager. According to Nancy Anton, who is a staffing professional and recruiter for a Fortune 100 company, throat clearing hurts your prospects during a job interview. "When I interview a person on the phone who keeps clearing their throat, I think that they are telling me something that is hard to swallow. Perhaps a lie or a half-truth or something they really don't like to say—such as repeating a pet answer to why they left a job. Sometimes they do a little laugh, then clear their throat, then start with the word, 'Honestly…' I really know this to be true when the throat clearing doesn't happen when they are on a subject that they are very comfortable and confident with. It seems to occur more with male candidates than with female candidates."

What can you do about habitual throat clearing? Read Chapter 5 of the book *Vocal Power: Harness Your Inner Voice to Conquer Everyday Communication Challenges*, by Arthur Samuel Joseph. He is truly a wealth of wisdom, knowledge, and solutions. You can also read his advice on a blog posted on my website dated March 24, 2017 entitled "Please don't clear your throat" featuring nine solutions on this throat clearing problem. When in doubt, swallow it.

> *Clearing your throat repeatedly during a networking meeting, a phone call, a presentation, or a job interview, can alienate your audience and cause them to doubt your expertise.*

It Sounds as if You're Not from Around Here

This brings up the topic of heavy accents and regional vocal traits. In addition to building rapport with others, we want to be understood easily. As the listener, we want to be careful not to judge people quickly or make them feel like an outsider. I remember living and working in Europe for three years. No matter how hard I tried to speak the British version of the English language, there wasn't a week that went by without some stranger asking me, "So, what part of America are you from?" This always made me feel like an outsider and not really welcome.

If you are someone who was born in a different country from the one where you are now living, you probably experience this vocal alienation effect even more than I did. Here are a few ideas that you might want to consider:

- **Be patient and forgiving of others.** Perhaps their exposure to the world is different from yours. You can help to educate them gently and work together to build a bridge of understanding, tolerance, and social justice.

- **Slow down your speech, and select words that you can confidently and clearly enunciate.** If there are words that trip you up or confuse other people, find a substitute. Simple words are best for communication.

- **Consider working with an accent modification coach.** A good coach can offer both in-person training and distance training for foreign-born professionals who need or want to modify their accent for the sake of clearer communication in English. I consider this type of professional development a career investment and one that shows tremendous motivation and awareness of yourself and your impact on others. To be an effective communicator, sometimes you need to do more than learn to read, write, and speak a different language

Can You Turn That Thing Down?

People are pretty sensitive to volume. My client Sharon told me that she keeps an extra bottle of aspirin in her desk drawer at work because her boss speaks so loudly. It gives her a headache; the volume creates physical pain for her. I imagine her boss is unaware of this negative effect she is having on a key member of her staff.

Other people speak so softly that they are hard to hear. You have to strain to take in what they are saying. Unless you are the big chief in the room and people are highly motivated (if not required) to listen to you, speaking too softly all the times can reduce your influence and communication effectiveness.

Giving Women a Voice

I have found that women, in particular, struggle with increasing the volume of their voices. Most of us were raised to be pleasant, cooperative, and quiet. Ladies don't raise their voices. This would be unladylike. Worse yet, we say nothing. We hold our tongue when really we have opinions and information that would bring value to the table. The other travesty about women and voice is that we don't use our voices when we really need them to protect ourselves.

My training as a martial artist has taught me that my voice is one of my greatest defense weapons. There is a fundamental difference between screaming (usually in a high pitch and from the throat) and yelling from the diaphragm. In the martial art of Tae Kwon Do, we are taught the *kihup* (pronounced key-up). This is the shouts or yells Tae Kwon Do students make when they do their kicks and punches. It's important to *kihup* with spirit and volume. It actually gives you extra physical power and has the effect of intimidating your attacker. This vocal technique is one of the first things we teach women when we conduct women's self-defense workshops. Some women are very uncomfortable doing this. They are not used to raising their voices. It scares them. If you are a woman reading this book right now, or if you have a wife, daughter, mother, girlfriend, or female colleague, please share this with them.

When you speak, you need to speak through, not speak at, your target. It's helpful to think of your voice soaring like an airplane successfully lifting off from an airport runway. Your voice, like that airplane, positively responds to the rules of aerodynamics. if you know how to work it. When you speak, see your voice leaving your lips and soaring up, up, and away. It lifts off and soars, and seems to go on forever. What you don't want to see or hear is your voice taking off only to come crashing down prematurely. That would be a really bad flight, and ineffective vocal delivery.

It's important that you take a few moments to warm up your voice before important phone calls, meetings, presentations, and interviews. If you do nothing else, get into the practice of gentle humming which will help to improve the vibrational quality of your voice when you speak. Doing a simple series of "Umm" and "Um Hmmm" sounds with your lips gently closed will help activate the vibration in the bone above your top lip. It should tickle a bit. Joseph calls this "finding the hub of your voice." One of the keys is the nasality of the sound you make in this exercise. You should feel a little vibration in your lips. Where the pitch ends up is optimally where you should end up speaking.

> *It's important that you take a few minutes to warm up your voice before important phone calls, meetings, presentations, and interviews.*

The Power of Silence

Perhaps my favorite dial on the vocal dashboard is the mute button. You know—the button on your phone that you press when you don't want anyone on the conference call to hear the sounds of your multitasking. All kidding aside, finding your mute button when you are communicating with people in person is a powerful discovery. There is power in the sound of silence. It creates space for people to consider what you have said. You don't have to fill every moment with new thoughts and ideas. What usually happens in this instance is that you fill them with comfort words like "Um" and "ah" and "so." Try saying nothing for a few seconds. Purposely say inside your head, "Stop talking now." Sit quietly and observe what's going on. Be comfortable and confident in this strategic break. Something magical may happen next. The other person may speak up and give you information that you wouldn't have garnered if you hadn't made space for it to come out in the discussion. Silence is golden.

There is a difference between awkward silence that makes people uncomfortable and purposeful silence that engages people on a conscious and unconscious level. You'll figure out the difference, but I want you to get comfortable even with the discomfort of silence. It always serves a purpose. It's like breathing; you couldn't live without it.

Now that you know how to build rapport with others, it's time to move on to figuring out how you can express your authentic self when you network. And that leads us to the next chapter where we'll cruise down the road called personal branding.

"People don't do business with you because you're a geek and can do regression in your head. They come to do business with you because they like you."
— JAMES LEE, VICE CHAIRMAN OF JPMORGAN CHASE & CO. (1997-2015)

9. My Way or the Highway

*How to Express Your Personal Brand
When You Network*

Like it or not, the car you drive says something about you. It is an expression of your personal brand. And just as there are many different styles, makes, models, and colors of cars, there are that many different kinds of networking styles. What's important is that your networking style and approach work for you, and reflect who you really are as a person. As people are different, you should expect to see different styles of networking from other people with whom you connect. That's part of the fun of networking.

While there are certainly business etiquette dos and don'ts that I would recommend that you follow, you still have a great deal of choice and creativity in how you network. There is no right or wrong way to do it. What really matters, however, is that you network consistently in order to build more mutually beneficial relationships before you need them.

But wouldn't it be nice if you could be more comfortable when you network? That you felt like yourself when you were doing it? That you weren't putting on an act and pretending to be someone that you're not? Good news! Sharing the authentic you and expressing your personal brand when you network can have a powerful, positive effect on you and the people you are connecting with.

What Is a Personal Brand?

We live in a branded world. Brands influence our buying decisions. We have relationships with brands—emotional attachments. We trust some and dislike others. They mean something to us: good, bad, and sometimes indifferent. They promise us something, and we expect them to live up to this every time. As rational and logical as we think we are, we are affected by brands in a deeply personal and emotional way.

The same holds true for people. We all have a personal brand and whether you know it or not, you already have one. It's encapsulated in your image, your identity, and your reputation. It's the unspoken promise that you make to the world, what people expect from you. The question is: Are you fully leveraging your personal brand? And are you living up to your personal brand with your daily interactions and behaviors?

The goal of a brand is to gain real estate in the gray matter of people's brains and the soft tissue of their hearts. We want you to think of us and love us so much that you choose us, prefer us over others, and recommend us often. Your personal brand needs to create a distinctive, ownable position in someone's mind.

> *What's important is that your networking style and approach work for you, and reflect who you really are as a person.*

Networking and Personal Branding Go Hand-in-Hand

A few years ago I invited personal branding expert Rahna Barthlemess, author of *Your Branding Edge: How Personal Branding Can Turbocharge Your Career*, to contribute to my blog. She wrote an illuminating piece titled "Networking and Personal Branding Go Hand-in-hand." Below is a short excerpt from her article. (You can read the entire article at americasmarketingmotivator.com/networking-and-personal-branding-go-hand-in-hand)

"How does your career advance? It is always through people—bosses who promote you, clients that hire you, consumers who buy from you, customers who rave about you, people who see and acknowledge your value. So it stands to reason that it's crucial to be connected with other people and to communicate with them in order to benefit from having a really strong personal brand.

Personal branding is a form of marketing yourself, becoming known by others for your strengths and your value. Strong personal branding helps your career because it paves the way for opportunities to come to you. So expand the list of people who know you and the value you can bring, as this will strengthen your personal brand.

Your branding edge is that "special something" that calls out to people that they need the unique value that you have to offer. The discipline of developing one's personal brand consists of identifying what is unique about you and then shining a spotlight on it so that others can see what value you have to bring.

Networking is a critical part of any personal brand and certainly a key aspect of turbocharging your career. You want people to know who you are and what you're all about, and you can do that in person, on the phone, at a networking event, or even digitally." — R. Barthlemess

But How Do You Do This?

It starts with deciding how you want to be known by others, as well as by yourself. This requires a high level of self-awareness. External feedback is also very useful, as is internal reflection. The closer your personal brand is to your authentic self, the easier it will be for you to express it consistently. It's very difficult to hold up a façade for long periods of time. Quite frankly, it's exhausting. And while we all need to improve things and correct shortcomings, the strength of our personal brand lies in our natural strengths, talents, passions and even our quirks.

Barthlemess suggests that your personal brand is your signature for success. She believes that if you know your personal brand, develop it and manage it consistently, then you have the opportunity to do only the work that you love for the rest of your life. "Living your personal brand should be as natural as breathing," states Barthlemess. "It's something you do every second of every day."

Here are the questions she has created that will help you discover your personal brand:

1. How would you describe yourself? List as many adjectives or qualities that you can think of. Ask other people to add to this list.

2. What are you really good at?

3. What do you like about yourself?

4. What don't you like about yourself?

5. Identify the major skills that you have.

6. What parts of your current work do you like and why?

7. What parts of your current work do you not like and why?

8. What are you really passionate about—what do you love to do?

9. What is your current work style?

10. What values do you hold dear professionally? Personally?

Taking time to answer these questions is a start to discovering your personal brand. You can read more on this topic by subscribing to her blog at RahnaBarthelmess.com

If you know your personal brand, develop it and manage it consistently, then you have the opportunity to do only the work that you love for the rest of your life.

Express Your Personal Brand When You Network

When you engage in networking, you are primarily representing yourself, even if you work for a particular company. People are first connecting with you, the human being. Who you work for is part of what you bring to the table in networking, but it's not the entire thing. Your employment is only one element of your packaging. The real product is on the inside—and that's you!

How to Become More Fluid and Natural in Networking

The secret to becoming more comfortable with networking is the same secret that will increase your success. It's called being authentically you. You must bring your whole human being to the table, not just the working-stiff part of you. Of course, some people won't like you, and that's okay. You don't have to be best friends with everyone.

If you allow yourself to be true, honest, and real, then you will more easily attract the people who are meant to be in your life. You will naturally repel the others who do not align well with your values and personality.

Dump the Duds

Not everyone you meet in the course of networking is going to be a great connection for you. You will have ideal connections and duds and a lot of people somewhere in the middle.

Identifying the duds is important because they will not bring out the best in you. They will waste your time, suck out your life force, and leave you with a taste of negativity for the whole process of networking. And we don't want this to happen, do we?

I was inspired by the concept of "dump the duds" after reading Michael Port's *Book Yourself Solid: The Fastest, Easiest, and Most Reliable System for Getting More Clients Than You Can Handle Even if You Hate Marketing and Sales*. Much of what Port talks about could be easily applied to networking rather than sales and marketing.

In his first chapter, entitled "The Red Velvet Rope Policy," Port suggests that we "dump the duds." That is, identify who isn't a good fit for you and purposefully let them go. I think this strategy is equally important in the networking process.

I'm thinking of one gentleman who was introduced to me by a mutual business associate. We got along well initially, and he eventually hired me to help him launch a new business venture. After working closely with him for a few months, we both discovered that we had very different styles and values. We mutually agreed to discontinue our professional work together. We haven't spoken in a number of years. He is still on my e-mail list, but neither of us is motivated to reconnect.

Upon reflection, I am grateful for this experience and for him for several reasons:

1. I discovered what a dud client for my business looks like. I'm sure I was a dud for him too. No doubt, we are ideal clients for someone else, just not each other.

2. I met other people through him, and they have turned out to be beneficial in my business and life.

3. I had the chance to test drive my very first motivational talk at one of his events. The filming of this talk turned into a number of videos that I posted on my YouTube channel. These videos have reached thousands of people around the globe. The value chain continues.

> *Some connections are better off as networking contacts rather than clients.*

Perhaps some connections are better off as networking contacts rather than clients. The relationship and expectations certainly change when money is exchanged. But underneath it all is the relationship. A strong one will withstand bumps in the road. A weak one will collapse under misunderstanding and conflict. Some connections are a misfit from the start.

The best approach in networking is to be you. Bring your authentic self into the networking relationship from the get-go. This way both of you will have the chance to see if this relationship will go anywhere. If it's not a fit, it's still a touch-point. You don't have to develop every networking connection into a mutually beneficial relationship. Be careful not to over-invest in dud clients and dud networking contacts. Move on and find those who complement your personal brand and goals.

Be fully present when you network. No facades. No distractions. But it's equally important that you are clear, focused, and purposeful in how you introduce yourself and how you engage people in productive conversations. Savvy networkers know how to express their personal brand in the context of their networking introduction. They know how to effectively position themselves for success. They practice and prepare their elevator pitch ahead of time. And that's the focus of our next chapter.

> *"Be more of yourself, and less of everybody else!"*
> — DAN SCHAWBEL, FOUNDER AND MANAGING PARTNER OF
> MILLENNIAL BRANDING, LLC

10. Construction Zone

*How to Perfect Your Pitch and Leverage
Purposeful Small Talk*

Everybody wants good roads, but no one likes driving through a construction zone. But the reality is that we must all adapt to changing conditions.

To become effective in networking, there is some construction that you'll need to endure. You need to learn how to position yourself quickly (in 30 seconds or less), how to strike up a conversation with someone you haven't met before in order to quickly find common ground, and how to move around to meet more people without being uncomfortable or looking like you are "working the room."

I call this process learning to "perfect your pitch." It involves the skill of introducing yourself in such a way that the other person asks you more questions and invites you to talk more. It's learning how to ask questions of others to learn more about them. These conversations are the beginnings of potential relationships. It's the stage where you get to know something about the other person, decide if you like that individual, and if he or she is interesting enough for a follow-up.

It is critical in this phase that you do not attempt to transact with this new person. Trying to sell your product or service at this startup phase of networking would severely shortchange the long-term potential of the relationship. Most people can smell a sales pitch from several yards away, and most people will immediately put their guard up toward you. Networking game over or at least penalty points issued.

I'd like you to repeat the following networking mantra: "Think relationships, not transactions; Think conversations, not sales pitches."

When networking with new people, I encourage you to suspend the urge to "sell" yourself or your products or services. Instead focus on getting to know each other. I've experienced job seekers so eager for work that they e-mail me with multiple attachments containing their resume and cover letters. This is too much too soon. It's a burden and a turn off. I recommend that you never e-mail your resume to someone until they specifically ask for it (e.g., "Please e-mail me your resume. I want to share it with someone who might know of an open position."), or after you get their permission to send it. (e.g., "May I e-mail you my resume so that you can share it with appropriate people in your network?")

Instead of pitching your wares, I want you to embrace the idea of purposeful small talk. It will help you lower their defenses and warm up the conversation and connection.

Purposeful Small Talk

Small talk is synonymous with chitchat, idle or trivial conversation. It is usually associated with the light informal conversation for social occasions such as, "We stood around making small talk until the guest of honor arrived." The small in this expression alludes to unimportant subjects of conversation, as opposed to serious or weighty ones. Most people tolerate small talk as part of civility, but few people I know actually enjoy it.

So how do you put more "purpose" into your small talk? How do you make this type of conversation more meaningful without trying to get overly heavy or intense too quickly?

> *"Think relationships, not transactions;*
> *Think conversations, not sales pitches."*

You find common ground. You make yourself approachable by putting a smile on your face. You get out of your own head and take more interest in other people. You realize that purposeful small talk is nothing more than an icebreaker to warm up the conversation so that you might have a shot at getting to know this person and possibly helping them (or vice versa).

Here's an example. I recently attended a special event hosted at the Connecticut General Assembly Legislative Office Building in Hartford. I came from another appointment and arrived early. They were just finishing setting up the event. Now I had a choice. I could "mingle" in a near-empty room, or I could hide in the cafeteria, pretending to be busy on my smartphone. I defaulted to the latter, but found it most unsatisfying, mostly because there were a few folks in the cafeteria who were having very loud conversations with their laptops (some sort of live meeting software). Frustrated with this forced eavesdropping (i.e., I couldn't not hear it as their conversation was so loud and public), I elected to pay a visit to the ladies room.

Wouldn't you know it, there were two other businesswomen in the bathroom. They were changing clothes and seemed in a hurry. The room was a bit hot and they were fanning themselves. I made a comment, telling them that the bathroom was indeed warm, but that the main lobby was much cooler. By asking another question, I learned that they had just set up the big display for the event.

When I moved into the main lobby, more people were starting to arrive for the event. I noticed one of the women from the bathroom was starting to greet guests. I walked over to her and commented how she cleaned up well and looked great in her white ruffled blouse and black pant suit. I introduced myself. Her name was Katherine Wiltshire and she was the Executive Director for the Connecticut Women's Hall of Fame. (Katherine has since retired from the CWHF.) This was her event. We had a lovely conversation, I learned more about her organization, and I told her a little about myself and what I did for a living. She expressed sincere interest; in fact, she commented, "Oh, I could really use your services."

Katherine introduced me to a few other guests who were arriving. We exchanged business cards. She invited me to attend their special event in November. I could see from the way she handled herself that Katherine was a woman of influence. She knows people. People know her. I'd like to meet more of her contacts. I made a mental note to myself, "Follow up and get to know Katherine better. She's a woman of influence."

What starts off as small talk can indeed lead to new possibilities. What makes small talk useful is when there is a bigger intention beyond it. Purposeful small talk helps you warm things up and can produce more mutually beneficial relationships. That, my friend, is one of the primary goals in networking.

> *Purposeful small talk helps you warm things up and can produce more mutually beneficial relationships.*

Learn to Ask More Interesting Questions

It has long been my belief that relationships start in conversation. In order for a contact to become a connection, you have to engage in a meaningful conversation. Good conversations help you find the common ground—perhaps a shared experience, belief, challenge, motivation, or goal. Therefore if you want more interesting conversations, then ask more interesting questions.

But it can be awkward starting a conversation with a stranger or speaking with someone that you don't know very well. This is the challenge that awaits you at networking events and meetings.

When networking with people at meetings, conferences, association meetings, or conventions, learn to ask more interesting open-ended questions to get the conversation going. Rather than the standard

"What do you do for a living?" ask a more creative, open-ended question to get a conversation going and enrich the human exchange.

You will learn more about the other person in a shorter amount of time. You also stand to find more common interests and deeper connections than you would if you only share your job descriptions. You may even learn something new about yourself and have fun in the process.

In my networking training workshops and keynote speeches, I've been experimenting with different types of questions to get the conversation going in speed networking exercises. I have developed a list of 40 interesting questions to get the conversation going. Here are a few of them:

1. What was the first paying job you held and how did it help prepare you for what you are doing now?

2. What was the most meaningful bit of career advice you've ever received (good or bad)?

3. What is one activity on your "bucket list" that you'd like to do in the next year or two?

4. Tell me about a risk have you taken recently that helped you to solve a problem.*

5. If you could change one thing about your work day, what would it be and why?

For the full list of questions, go to the Open Vault section of my website and download the free workbook, "A Guide to Networking Conversation Starters."

---

* **Footnote:** Question four with the asterisk is courtesy of Jenny Drescher and Ellen Ornato, of ConnectAndImprov. They believe that people "connect at the level of who." This philosophy is simple: if you had ten conversations with ten people who had identical jobs and titles, what would stand out about them? What you'd remember would be who they are as individuals, not jobs, because real connection occurs human-to-human, not title-to-title. Check out their very cool workshops were you can learn the art of "business improv" at connectandimprov.com

> *If you want more interesting conversations, then ask more interesting questions.*

So here's what you do. After you have shaken hands and exchanged names, try asking one of these questions to start the conversation. To ease into the question, you might want to preface it with a softening phrase and inclusion of their first name. For example, "I'm curious [their first name]...." or "[their first name], I have a question for you...." I know what you are thinking: these questions are awfully personal and may be awkward to ask when first meeting someone. It's true, but I've seen these questions work time and time again. They help to bypass the purposeful small talk and allow you to fast forward to more energizing discussion. They also allow you to identify "common ground" and shared experiences that otherwise might never be unearthed.

Let me give one such example. I was teaching an advanced networking class to a group of high potential talent who worked at a large insurance company based in Hartford, Connecticut. The employees had flown in from all parts of the nation to participate in the professional development program. They also had the opportunity to meet and greet top company executives who were vested in developing the talent bench and leadership pipeline of the organization. I arrived early and had the chance to sit in on a small group discussion with one executive named Walter. At first, the participants were asking Walter the safe and expected questions, such as "How's the strategy going?" and "What do you think will happen when the new regulations take hold?" Walter politely answered these questions, as he no doubt had done a dozen times before. I decided to jump in and ask Walter one of the networking conversation starters. "Walter, I'm curious, what was your first paying job, and how did it prepare you for the work world?" Walter's physiology immediately shifted and he was engaged. He told the group a fascinating story about working in a cornfield as a teenager.

He then shared some personal information about his volunteer work coaching middle school ice hockey teams. Walter also said to me, "That's a really excellent question. I think I'll use that question with the next job candidate I interview." What I observed in this round table discussion was the power and energy created by taking a risk and asking a more interesting question. Don't be boring and stick with only the safe questions, such as 'What brought you here today?" Take a risk and ask a more interesting question. You may just find you learn more, engage more, and connect more quickly and deeply.

What Makes a Good Networking Introduction?

Few people I know enjoy giving their 30-second elevator pitch. It can be one of the most aerobic parts of your day: heart pounding, palms sweating, inner dialogue on haywire. And that starts happening about 10 minutes before you have to say word one.

To calm yourself down and reduce the anxiety about the whole thing, I suggest you tell yourself, "This is just practice" every time you give your networking introduction. This type of communication is fluid, flexible, and forgiving! Give yourself a break, and lighten up on the pressure. Try to breathe.

The goal of your networking is to position yourself and to get the other person's permission to talk more. If you hear that individual reply, "Tell me more" or "That's interesting, how do you do that?" then you have done well. Creating curiosity, interest, and rapport is a key outcome that you should seek when you introduce yourself in networking situations.

The best networking introductions do five things really well. I call these the "MR ABE" criteria. If you can learn to dial up these five elements of your elevator pitch, you will be moving forward toward greater networking confidence and results:

M = memorable

R = relatable or relevant

A = authentically you

B = believable and credible

E = engaging and energized

Let's examine each one of these points, and figure out how we can construct your elevator pitch with these elements in place.

(Listen to audio samples and download a free workbook to help you craft and perfect your elevator pitch at americasmarketingmotivator. com/mr-abe-test)

> *You meet many people in the course of your life. Some stand out; some don't. Some people's names you can remember; others you don't.*

Make Yourself More Memorable

You meet many people in the course of your life. Some stand out; some don't. Some people's names you can remember; others you don't. You, my friend, want to strive to be one of those memorable people. To do this, you must seek to be sticky. By this, I mean that you must find something about you (positive) that people can easily remember. Many people are visual and will link your face to your name. Others may remember you based on something compelling you said or did (again, hopefully positive).

Your challenge is to decide ahead of time how you want to be remembered. What do you want to "stick?" Is it your name? Is it your occupation? Is it your personal passion?

Here's the deal with stickiness and memory. If you attempt to tell your whole life story or every detail about everything you do, offer, or have, nothing will stick. You must focus and be purposeful.

If you have a difficult-to-pronounce name, you might want to teach people how to say it. If they are unsure about how to pronounce your name, they will avoid it altogether. It's too awkward and uncomfortable. So, give them an easy way to remember your name. Here are two examples.

I met a woman whose name was Cauna. She said it quickly and I looked at her business card, but it didn't stick. I was suddenly uncomfortable with asking her for her name (again). We got into a discussion about teaching people how to pronounce your name, and she shared this with me, "My name is Cauna, pronounced like Kona coffee." I instantly smiled as I conjured up images of Hawaii and the delicious taste of Kona coffee. Cauna has anchored her name on something very positive and stimulated a multiple sensory experience for me in an instant. I followed up by sending her a card with a picture of coffee beans. I will always remember her and say to myself, "Cauna, like the Kona coffee."

Mind you, Cauna was a trust officer with a major bank. She was not in the coffee business. But this doesn't matter. What does matter is that I can now confidently pronounce her name and will remember her. She has made it easier for me to get to know her. How can you help people pronounce your name correctly? How can you help people remember you?

How Can You Be More Relevant?

People don't listen to you until you have captured their attention. This holds true for parents, teachers, bosses, and networkers. Even if you have a position of authority, you will experience a difference between people who hear you, listen to you, and engage with you. The key is how relevant you are to them, how much they can relate to you, and how much you can relate to them. I like to define relevance as "I need you right now." In fact, I often ask myself this key question when thinking about connecting with my clients and prospects: "How can I be more relevant right now?"

In networking, relevance is what happens when people connect to what you are saying, because they can relate to it. You have found common ground and now have more to talk about.

Here's a fun approach to practice in a more formal networking setting, like chambers of commerce meetings. Before you say your name, ask a question. Get the people to go inside themselves and answer the question (or relate to the problem/experience you have just opened with).

Need a few examples of how this works?

- Anyone here have a messy desk? My name is Linda and I'm a professional organizer. I help busy professionals and business owners reclaim time and space in their lives and businesses by creating organizational systems that work for them. Linda— your professional organizer.

- Do you remember the "Peanuts" cartoon where Lucy, Linus, and Charlie Brown are shown in the classroom? You never see the teacher, but you know that she's there because when she speaks, the kids hear (audience will answer "wha, wha, wha"). My name is Tammy and I'm a marketing consultant. I help business professionals like you take the blah-blah-blah out of your marketing speak. Tammy—your marketing consultant.

- When was the last time you sat through a really boring PowerPoint presentation? How excruciating was it? My name is Kathy and I'm an executive presentation coach. I help business professionals reduce their PowerPoint clutter so they better engage their audience and move them to action. Kathy—your executive presentation coach.

The beauty of this approach is that you say your name only after you have their attention. They are more likely to remember your name and pay attention to what you have to say. This is a creative way to become more relevant when you introduce yourself in networking situations.

Authenticity Means Being Comfortable in Your Own Skin

How much conviction do you have in what you are saying? If the level is high, then your physiology or body language will back you up. Your nonverbal and verbal communication will be congruent. If your conviction is low—if, for example, you don't like the company you work for, but you are forced to give the company "spiel"—then your body language will give you away instantly. You will not come across as being comfortable in your own skin.

Have you ever witnessed this situation? Someone is talking about what he or she does for a living, and the conversation is pretty matter-of-fact. Then suddenly that person comes alive and gets animated, sharing with you something he or she is passionate about—perhaps a special project, a charity, an issue.

That person's entire physiology shifts as he or she becomes totally transformed with passion and energy. What just happened? (And how do we make this happen earlier in the conversation, interview, or meeting?)

By sharing what you are passionate about when you network, the chances of a stronger connection increase substantially. You bring your entire human being to the party, not just the working-stiff part. I encourage you to share more of yourself when you network. Now, of course, there are topics that may be a bit dangerous (religion, politics, sex). Perhaps these topics are best put on hold until a deeper relationship is established.

William Shakespeare wrote, "To thine own self be true." This is a great philosophy when it comes to personal branding and to expressing your personal brand when you network with others.

If you attempt to be something or someone that you are not, or try to put on a professional façade when networking, you will quickly become exhausted and discovered. Your body language will give you away. Strive to be more authentic when you network, and watch how this improves your conversations, connections, and relationships!

Believability: Are You the Real Deal?

The flip side of the authenticity coin is believability. How credible are you? Do you look, sound and act the part? If you are a health coach, and show up drinking a Coca-Cola and eating a donut, you may send a mixed message.

You can't control what other people think, but you can influence it. When networking, don't brag, but remember to let people know about your experiences and credentials. Sometimes these are best showcased through client stories. Talk about whom you have worked with and what kind of problems you helped them solve. This will get the wheels turning about the value you can create for them and others they know.

Have someone else introduce you, and let them brag about you. This is the power of public relations and third-party endorsement. It's a subtle form of social proof. You can maintain your modesty and humbleness while being positioned as an accomplished person.

The other aspect to consider when dialing up your credibility is your visual and vocal presentation. How you dress and how you use your voice will either build you up or break you down in other people's eyes. Human beings form judgments about other people in a blink of an eye. Your credibility and believability may be well served by powering up your professional image: polished shoes, clean fingernails, underwear that remains under your clothes, shirts and blouses that don't distract with too much skin showing, and clothes that actually fit your body (tailoring is a great investment in your professional image).

> *William Shakespeare wrote, "To thine own self be true." This is a great philosophy when it comes to personal branding and to expressing your personal brand when you network with others.*

Start paying more attention to how you end your sentences. You learned in Chapter 8 about the dangers of Upspeak. You know that your voice inflection can change the communication. By changing how you vocalize a sentence, you can alter the meaning of it as perceived by the listener. With the same sentence and same words, you can make it sound like you are asking a question, stating a fact, or commanding someone to do something. There will be times when you'll want to use all three of these voice inflection techniques.

You can put more confidence and authority into your voice by using the "low and slow" command tonality. Lowering the pitch of your voice (within your natural range) has other added benefits. It has the effect of slowing you down, thereby encouraging more precise articulation of each word. It also tends to minimize any nasal vocal quality, which many listeners find annoying.

- Statement: Word ➡ Word ➡ Word (all words spoken with same emphasis)

- Question: Word ➡ Word ➹ Word (last word ends on a higher pitch note)

- Command: Word ➡ Word ➘ Word (last word spoken with lower tone of voice)

Bring More Positive Energy into the Conversation

Many people have some anxiety around the topic of networking (similar to the fear of public speaking). As a result, their energy levels are diminished or altered in some unfavorable way. And people feel your energy. It either attracts them toward you or repels them away from you. Sometimes the impact is neutral, with no major gravitational pull either way. This doesn't help your networking efforts.

It's time to put more energy into your networking. It starts with your attitude and how you are thinking. Brain research continues to prove that we are all neurologically wired. What we think impacts how we feel, which impacts our physiology and what goes on with our bodies. Change any one of these forces (thoughts, feelings, physiology), and you affect the other two.

This is why laughter can make such a big difference in your life. You are changing your physiology, which alters your state and shifts your mindset. It is also highly contagious—in a positive way!

The next time you network, try smiling and laughing a bit more. It will increase your engagement level and make the whole experience a lot more fun for you and others!

{ *You can put more confidence and authority into your voice by using the "low and slow" command tonality.* }

Eye Contact

I want you to think about the power of eye contact. When we are nervous, we are more likely to look down or look away. Think about what happens when you are walking down a city street. You see someone coming towards you, your eyes meet, you are getting closer to each other, ready to pass by, and someone diverts eyes down or away. Hmmm. What would happen if you held the eye contact, smiled, and said "hello?" You might make someone's day. You might stand up a bit taller. You might get a confidence boost. Your energy level just went up, my friend.

Let me remind you that people can see when you have wandering eyes. They notice when you look away from them and when you are scanning the room for "better opportunities." This may be unconscious on your part, but it sends a very clear signal to other people that they don't matter to you that much. When you are networking with someone, show that person respect by giving your full attention. Look that person in the eye, and be with him or her, even if just for a short time. This will help improve your connection and create the opportunity for a networking relationship to develop.

Handshakes (again)

I addressed the topic of handshakes in Chapter 5 "Road Grime and Door Dings," but it is so important that I bring it up again in this section. Nothing bugs me more than a weak, incomplete handshake. Whether from a man or a woman, I feel sad and disappointed when someone puts a limp fish hand in mine. Of course, there's the opposite problem—too much force, too much pressure. You are now hurting me physically. That doesn't help to build rapport.

In my networking skills workshops, we actually practice giving and receiving professional handshakes. I know this sounds remedial, but people need to practice and get honest feedback. There are too many crappy handshakes happening. We need to up our performance on this critical business greeting.

The difficult part about a handshake is that it happens so quickly. You have a split second to figure out what kind of handshake would work best for the other person you are networking with. How do you know how much pressure to apply? I suggest that you read the other person's body language, and allow your kinesthetic sense to guide you. Don't assume that all women prefer a softer handshake. There are tennis players and other female athletes who have a very firm handshake. If you overdo it or underdo it, you can always ask to redo that handshake. "Let's try that again" can be a great thing to say if the first time didn't work so well.

And then there are those who feel compelled to hug you. What do we do with the huggers?

Hugging and Kissing

Clients often ask me whether it's appropriate to hug and kiss when greeting people. This one is hard because I am a very huggy type of person, but I have also learned the lesson that it is not always appropriate. Let me share an embarrassing personal story with you.

I was in Germany coordinating a European trade show on behalf of my company. I had been living in England for two years working with all our offices around Europe. It was pretty confusing for a young American to figure out the right number of kisses.

I was meeting two gentlemen from a German trade show company for the first time. One gentleman was quite large—at least three times my size. I suddenly questioned myself, not knowing what the proper greeting for this situation was. In a panic, I walked over to the German man, shook his hand and gave him a kiss on the right cheek and one on the left. I pulled back only to see him blush. I looked over at the other German man and could see him laugh and smile. He was ready for his. Cultural faux pas!

In the end, this was harmless, but it sure has stuck with me for many years. There are nuances from culture to culture and country to country that must be studied and understood in advance. How much touching? What kind of touch? How much personal space? Even eye contact rules are different. When in doubt, ask.

Alan Pease, author of *The Definitive Book of Body Language*, has this to say about international greeting norms:

> "The Scandinavians are happy with a single kiss, the French most prefer a double, while the Dutch, Belgians, and Arabs go for a triple kiss. The Australians, New Zealanders, and Americans are continually confused about greeting kisses and bump noses as they fumble their way through a single peck. The Brits either avoid kissing by standing back or will surprise you with a European double kiss."

Oh, and Japan—no touching, as bodily contact is considered impolite. Japanese people bow on first meeting with the holder of the highest status bowing the least and the one with the lowest status bowing the most.

And Germany? It's on the "don't touch" list, according to Dr. Ken Cooper, author of *Bodybusiness: The Sender's and Receiver's Guide to Nonverbal Communication.*

Do your research in advance, so that you can avoid any embarrassing situations. Or make it your policy that you don't hug or kiss on the first networking meeting. Get to know each other well before you get that close.

Now that you've figured out how to introduce yourself in networking situations, and have practiced and received feedback on your verbal and nonverbal performance, it's time to learn what you can do to stand out from the crowd by going the extra mile.

> *"The road to success is always under construction."*
> — LILY TOMLIN, AMERICAN ACTRESS, COMEDIAN AND PRODUCER

11. Going the Extra Mile

*Showing Up and Following Up are the
Keys to Your Success*

Have you ever been driving on the highway and became worried that you missed the exit? Maybe you are not exactly sure where this destination is, but your gut tells you that you've already passed it. When this happens to me, I remind myself to stay the course. My destination is just around the bend. Call this persistence if you will, but it is spooky how often it turns out to be true. Turning around prematurely is counterproductive. You must have faith that the destination lies ahead. You must go that extra mile.

The same holds true in networking. Sometimes new connections you make don't immediately pan out. They do not appear to produce the great results that you had hoped for or were led to believe would happen by the person who connected you. Now is the time to stay the course and not abandon this new relationship prematurely. It could help take you to great new places if you give the relationship the time to develop.

How do you make this happen? First you show up, and then you practice systematic follow-up. Let me give you an example of how these two guiding principles of networking helped me create a powerful networking relationship that otherwise would not have been available to me. It's the story of how I met Juli Ann Reynolds, then CEO of the Tom Peters consulting company, and how I developed a professional networking relationship with her. This relationship continues to produce value in my life and business to this day.

> *Sometimes new connections you make don't immediately pan out. Now is the time to stay the course and not abandon this new relationship prematurely. It could help take you to great new places if you give the relationship the time to develop.*

Lesson No. 1: You Must Show Up, Even if It Is Against All Odds

Several years ago, I belonged to the MENG association, which stands for Marketing Executive Networking Group. My friend Shirley had recommended that I join this group to help support my new business launch as a marketing consultant. One particular meeting was being held in Boston, which entailed a three-hour drive each way for me, and the meeting was at night. I had made arrangements to travel with my friend Shirley to the meeting, but she canceled on me at the very last minute. I remember being parked at the gas station making the decision to continue without her to the meeting. I'm not a very good night driver. I get sleepy, and I get lost a lot, especially in new areas. However, I was pretty motivated to go since Juli Ann Reynolds was the speaker and the group was discussing the power of personal branding.

On my way to Boston, I almost turned back three separate times. In fact, I was within one mile of the meeting, but could not find the building within the Charlestown Naval Yard. I flagged down a police officer and even he did not know. So there I was, so close but yet so lost. I overcame my fear and recommitted to showing up. I had come too far to turn back now. I parked the car and went door to door, asking strangers for directions until I found the building.

Did I mention that I was ninety minutes late to the meeting? And it was scheduled to be only a two-hour meeting. But I walked in, made my apologies for being tardy and quickly found a seat and began to participate in the very interesting discussion.

After the meeting, I made a point to introduce myself to Juli Ann, shake her hand, and exchange business cards with her. I thanked her for hosting the MENG meeting at her swanky urban offices. It was a great evening all the way around.

Lesson No. 2: You Must Follow Up with People You Meet

A few days later, I rang Juli Ann and thanked her again. I told her what I had taken away from her talk and what I intended to do with the information. I then asked her if she would be willing to network with me from time to time. She accepted.

During a period of six months, we touched base a few times. She was very good at returning my phone calls. She even invited me up to the office to meet a few of her colleagues. They were looking for motivated marketing consultants to help them grow their training and consulting business. She even invited me to participate in a special train-the-trainer workshop for their "Brand You!" program. I attended this two-day event and met more interesting people who have since become part of my professional network.

Several months later, she called me and asked if I would do a motivational talk for one of their clients who was having a sales meeting in Mystic, Connecticut. That was a paid speaking gig!

I brought her a prospective business opportunity that I was developing for a John Deere dealership chain in the South. Interestingly, Juli Ann grew up on a farm in Nebraska, so she could relate to much of the John Deere world. Unfortunately, the timing of our proposal coincided with the U.S. economic meltdown in 2008-2009, so the opportunity was put on hold.

Later that year, I had the opportunity to introduce Juli Ann to Diane, a client of mine who runs a national insurance company. Juli Ann and Diane reminded me of each other. They were both women, about the same age, both CEOs of companies, and they had both broken through the glass ceiling and not only survived, but succeeded, in male-dominated industries. They even looked alike. So naturally, I thought to connect them.

Within two weeks of my introduction, they had spoken on the phone. They both are clearly motivated networkers and understand the power and importance of expanding your professional network. Even when you are at the top of your career game, you need a robust professional network to continue to build your success and opportunity.

When I think back on this story, it occurs to me that it would not have been possible if I hadn't pushed through my own internal barriers and made the effort to show up. Staying at home or staying in the office day and night will not help you grow your professional network. There is a great deal of benefit to be had from getting out of the office regularly.

This story also illustrates the importance of follow-up. I wonder how many people at that MENG meeting actually reached out to Juli Ann after the meeting and set a course to develop a relationship with her. I might have been the only one to do so. This is why I recommend that you always make the effort to introduce yourself to the speaker. These are the kinds of subject-matter experts that you want to add to your circle of influence. Think about this (and act upon it) the next time you go to a meeting, conference, or convention.

Years in the Making

I've been curious about how staying in touch through time pans out to create networking and business success. The following personal story from my networking friend, Chris Amorosino, inspired me. Chris is a copywriter extraordinaire with an intriguing approach to business writing which he outlines in "Writing Business Stories That Live Profitably Ever After." The same could be said about the magic of staying in touch with people in your network.

Networking fairy tales do come true. Here's one such example from Chris:

> "Years ago I was a lowly newsletter writer at a trade association when a senior vice president (SVP) walked into my tiny cubicle. This leader was someone everyone in my department admired. We thought he'd end up being president of the association one day. He had never been in my cubicle before, and since I was not part of his division, his visit was curious.
>
> The SVP began quizzing me about book publishing. After ten minutes or so, I stopped him and tried to ask politely why he was asking me all these questions. He told me that he planned to write a book one day and was doing some fact gathering.
>
> I never forgot that. If this intelligent, talented senior executive was writing a book and was asking me for information, I planned to stay in touch. About a year later, the SVP left the association. I would call him every six months or so to ask if he was ready to start on his book. He never was.
>
> A few years later, I left the association. Still, I kept in touch with the former SVP. Now in the age of e-mail, I would shoot him a message every so often to ask about the book inside his head. More than eight years after our first conversation, the SVP contacted me to say he was ready to write his book. It took three-and-a-half years after that day to write and publish the 20-chapter book. But what a great project!
>
> I got to work with a very smart person. He allowed me to add some enhancements to his book, including eight cartoons and one chapter. When the book arrived from the press, I felt as close as a man can feel to giving birth. What a great feeling!

Perhaps this isn't a pure networking story, but it does speak to one basic of networking: staying in touch. You never know when a prospect or client is going to need you. You always want to be top of mind. I earned a nice paycheck on that project and received follow-up work. But better yet was the thrill of helping someone spread the wealth of his knowledge to a wide audience. As I write this, I can look three feet to my left and see that book sitting on my shelf. Life is good."

Chris' networking success took eleven years to incubate before it manifested into business success. Do you have that kind of patience and faith?

> *Staying at home or staying in the office day and night will not help you grow your professional network.*

Consistency Pays Off

Woody Allen got it mostly right in his famous quote, "Eighty percent of success is showing up." I like to think follow-up is the remaining twenty percent of the success quotient.

Absenteeism, whether literal or figurative, doesn't do much for your visibility and connection to the community. While showing up is critical in networking and relationship building, you must go the extra mile with timely and consistent follow-up. There are serious goodies and rewards to be gained through networking as long as you practice patience and disciplined follow-up. I like to think that those who show up, go up, and those who follow up, go up in growth.

I know what you are thinking. Showing up and following up are easier said than done. It's like being a professional race car driver. They make it look so easy. We can envision ourselves zooming around the racetrack at top speeds without injury to vehicle or person. But make no mistake, it's a high level skill that few people possess and even fewer can maintain over time. Our next chapter will guide you through designing a system that will enable you to consistently, effectively, and efficiently follow up and stay in touch with important people in your network. Fasten your seat belts.

> *"The world is run by those who show up."*
> — ROBERT B. JOHNSON, *JOURNAL OF MANAGEMENT IN ENGINEERING* — JANUARY/FEBRUARY 1999

12. Drive an Automatic

How to Systematize Your Follow-Up

There's a reason that most new cars are built and sold with automatic transmissions. It makes driving a car easier. You have to perform fewer steps in order to commandeer and control the vehicle. Of course, some manual transmission buffs don't believe this is real driving (and that repair costs can actually be higher). But I hope you'll agree with me that the fewer steps you have to remember, the easier the process.

When it comes to networking, the task of follow-up can overwhelm people and create actual stress in their lives. They are bombarded with business cards that they don't know what to do with, and phone calls and e-mails that they don't have time to make or answer. They are already overbooked with their job and family responsibilities. Who has time to stay in touch?

I have a solution for this classic dilemma. You need to create an organized, systematic method of networking follow-up. I suggest that you employ the THERAPY model of motivated networking follow-up. Here's what's involved:

> **T = Targeted:** You must put some targeting strategy into your networking game plan.
>
> **H = Helpful:** Find simple, creative, and time-efficient ways to be more helpful to the people in your professional network.
>
> **E = Efficient:** Whatever system you plan to use, it must be highly efficient; otherwise you won't do it consistently.
>
> **R = Reliable:** You must strive to be highly reliable with your

networking follow-up. You must fulfill the promises that you make in a timely and consistent manner.

A = Accessible: You must make yourself easily "findable" for the people in your network. Your full contact details must be available to them.

P = Personalized: To break through the clutter, your networking follow-up must be personalized. It must feel like it could only be from you, and only for them.

Y = Yippee, Yahoo!: You should have fun with your follow-up. It can be something that brings joy and creates energy in your life and others' lives as well.

Let's break down each one of these factors and figure out how to incorporate it into your networking follow-up system. This will allow you to drive your professional network more easily and more effectively.

Targeted Networking

In Chapter 3, "What Road to Take," we discussed the importance of identifying who in your network is the most important to you. Who can help you get the farthest fastest? Which relationships are most critical to your life, career, and business? This is where you need to spend the majority of your networking time and energy. They are the pistons in the engine of your professional network. They help you keep things cranking along.

To take care of these important relationships, your follow-up needs to be more frequent and special. They matter to you. Don't ignore them or take them for granted. Check in with them every five weeks or so. Offer to help them in any way you can. Introduce them to people that they want to meet. Cultivate and develop these top relationships over time. Spend quality face time with them.

The other aspect about targeting is knowing who doesn't add

value to your network. Yes, know who your "duds" are, and limit the amount of time and energy you devote to them. You can do this gently and even indirectly, but limit the time you spend with them. Here's where no follow-up is a good strategy. You have decided not to encourage this relationship, not to develop it further. This is a perfectly acceptable thing to do. It fact, it is often a smart decision. Don't invest your time and energy in people and relationships that bring you down or pull you back. They can be poisonous to your professional and personal development (they may even be in your immediate family or close circles).

Now that you are targeted with your networking strategy, we can move on to how you can use your time and energy creatively to be helpful (and valuable) to the people in your professional network.

Being Helpful is Easier than You Think

Networking is about building and maintaining mutually beneficial relationships before you need them. So how do you add more benefit to your networking? How can you be more helpful to other people without making it a demanding full-time, Good Samaritan, extra job?

My first idea for you is to stop sending all of those e-mails. Swear off the "reply all" button. Many busy professionals that I know get 100 or more e-mails every day. They are overwhelmed by the sheer sight of their inbox. Your well-intended e-mail follow-up is not a gift; it feels more like a burden. You need to give more thought to the other person and how that person likes to be communicated with, not just to what's convenient for you.

Here are some creative ideas on how you can be more helpful to the people in your professional network:

1.   Connect them with someone in your network who you think can help them.

2.   Write a recommendation on LinkedIn.

3. Leave them short, clear, and concise voice mails, and remember to include your phone number (say it slowly twice).

4. Send them articles that you read and think might be of interest to them.

5. Send them a gift card to Dunkin' Donuts or Starbucks with a short message, "Enjoy a coffee on me."

6. Alert them if you find a typo in their materials or in their online profile. Of course, do this gently and without judgment. You want them to look good.

7. Send them a copy of your favorite professional development book or resource.

8. Keep them motivated by sending messages of support and encouragement.

9. Congratulate and acknowledge their accomplishments.

10. Alert them to any news or information about their company or industry. You want them to be "in the know."

11. If you have a website or blog offer them the opportunity to contribute a guest article. Feature their expertise with your visitors and fans.

12. Alert them of upcoming events they may be interested in. Invite them to join you. You don't have to pay their way; you just want them to have the same opportunity that you have.

13. Share your "lessons learned" with them.

14. Help them think through a current challenge. Let them pick your brain.

15. Offer them candid and constructive feedback. Always secure their permission first. Unsolicited feedback can sometimes backfire. Start by asking the question "Are you open to some feedback?" or "Would you like some feedback on that?"

16. Let them know if you see an interesting job opening that they or someone in their network may want to know about.

17. Share best practices and coach each other.

18. Offer to play the role of their accountability partner. Find out what their major goal is, what is keeping them from accomplishing it and offer to hold them accountable to a specific deadline. Structure this arrangement so it works for both of you.

19. Help them learn more about their personal brand. Tell them what you admire most about them and how they are uniquely different from other people.

Efficiency Is Essential for Your Follow-Up Success

I believe disorganization will kill you, and it will be a slow, painful death. You can avoid it by putting some organization, discipline, and efficiency into how you approach your networking follow-up. The good news is that even if this is not part of your DNA, you can hire outside professional organizers to help you improve in this area.

When it comes to increasing the efficiency of your networking follow-up system, you need to have a web-based contact management system to organize and update the many connections you will make through your networking. I recommend having one online system so you can access it 24/7 from anywhere in the world. The old Rolodex system, with the spinning racks that held the business cards, was a terrific solution in its day, but now we have more advanced technology to help us take our organization to the next level of efficiency and access. Excel spreadsheets are good, but there are better systems out there that you should be investigating. Technology is changing daily, so keep current on the latest tools that might help you improve your follow-up system.

Shop around, and ask other people you know which contact management system they use and what they like and dislike about it. You might consider a CRM (customer relationship management) system. While these systems typically are designed to support the sales process, they may offer you some additional functionality that could boost your productivity and efficiency when it comes to networking follow-up.

It's important to note that you'll need to collect complete contact information from the people you meet in networking. E-mail addresses are not enough. You should record phone numbers and mailing addresses—even birthdays and other relevant personal information. This becomes important as you build closer relationships over time. The contact management system you select must accommodate your future needs as well as your immediate ones.

So where do you have your contact information now? Is it scattered all over your desk? Do you have bundles of business cards held together by rubber bands tucked away in your office? Do you have contacts stored in your e-mail and on your cell phone? It's time to consolidate all this information. If you are feeling overwhelmed and don't know where to start, consider hiring a virtual assistant. Interview a few of them. And, yes, pay that person out of your own pocket. Your current disorganization is costing you more than you know. It's time to get organized and efficient with the people in your professional network.

> *Every time you follow up on a promise you've made to someone else, you are putting pennies into the equity bank of your professional reputation.*

How Reliable Are You?

The golden rule in networking is: If you offer to help someone, you must fulfill that promise promptly and completely. If you don't, your professional reputation may be at risk. You don't want to be known as a ball-dropper or someone who talks a good game, but doesn't come through in the end.

I know that most of us don't set out to be unreliable; it often happens because life is very demanding and everyone wants a piece of our time and attention. Our intention is to help others, and sometimes, in our enthusiasm, we make promises that are very difficult to fulfill. Overpromising and under-delivering in any context are damaging to your reputation.

Here's one possible solution: If, during the course of networking with someone, you can think of multiple connections for that person, ask which one of these introductions would be most useful right now. Force that person to make a choice. If he or she says all of them, gently suggest picking one connection to start. After completing this connection, the individual can contact you to get the next introduction. This method helps focus all parties and reduces the possibility of anyone being overwhelmed, and the risk of inaction. Even job-seekers can get overwhelmed with a list of three to five people they need to contact following your meeting.

The final suggestion I have to help you improve your reliability in networking is to make it a greater priority. Every time you follow up on a promise or offer that you have made to someone else, you are putting pennies into the equity bank of your professional reputation. These small investments compound and multiply over time. Your relationship and your results from networking will also be elevated.

Make Yourself Easily Accessible

Unless you are in the witness protection program, you will want to be found by other people, old friends and new friends alike. I realize that some people are more private in nature and don't like to promote themselves. Even in these cases, you can help the people in your close personal circles get in touch and stay in touch with you more easily by keeping your contact information updated and easily available to them. Don't make them go hunting for your contact details. Don't leave voice mails without leaving your name and phone number. Don't send e-mails without a signature that has your contact information.

Why? Because I might just want to get in touch with you, but the thought of searching for your contact information might be enough to let this opportunity pass me by. By making yourself more easily "findable," you increase the chances of people returning your phone calls, responding to you, and staying in touch with you.

If you leave one job and start another, please let me know. Send me your new contact details. Don't allow yourself to fall off my radar. Help me keep track of you and all the exciting (or not so exciting) changes in your life.

How can you be more accessible online? Open an account on LinkedIn and Facebook. For you more advanced social media mavens, get a Twitter or Instagram account. Put these links in your e-mail signature so they are automatically posted every time you send me an e-mail. Put a photo that I recognize (current and professional) on your profile pages. I went to search for my Uncle Carlos Garcia on LinkedIn. Thankfully, he had a professional photo portrait on his profile; otherwise it would have been difficult for me to find him. Do you know how many Carlos Garcia's there are in America? Please don't put your baby picture, or photos of your kids or your horse on your profile. I won't recognize you as easily. Your efforts to be cute create difficulty and sometimes mistrust for me. Put your real face with your real name. Now I can find you.

How can you be more accessible offline? When using the traditional communication channels, such as phone and "snail mail," remember to put your return address and return phone number. Think about your voice mail recorded greeting. In fact, call yourself now, and listen to it. Is it professional? Does it provide all the information I need to get hold of you? Do you have energy in your voice that will motivate me to leave a message and get in touch with you? Or do you sound like the living dead?

> *By making yourself more easily "findable," you increase the chances of people returning your phone calls, responding to you, and staying in touch with you.*

How can you be more accessible for face-to-face interaction? Make time for me. Feed me. As author Keith Ferrazzi says in his fabulous, highly recommended book on networking, you should *Never Eat Alone*. Make connections with people in your network when you are refueling yourself. Share lunch, meet for breakfast, or have dinner with them. While I appreciate that this can be very time consuming and expensive, relationships are enhanced with quality face time. If food is a negative issue, then meet for a walk and get exercise together. If golf is a passion, then meet at the driving range after work, and shoot a bucket of balls together or play nine holes. Meet for a manicure or pedicure. Whatever it is that you enjoy and allows you to spend quality time with the people you care about, make time to do it together.

The last idea I have for you about making yourself accessible in face-to-face situations is rideshare together. Don't drive alone to conferences and meetings. Rather, arrange to drive together. You will have concentrated time to chat and catch up and get to where you need to be—together! Not only will you save gas and lighten up your carbon footprint, you will enhance your networking relationships.

Get Personal with Your Networking Follow-Up

Whether you have a formal or informal follow-up style, you can develop closer relationships with your networking contacts by sharing more of yourself with them. Every time you follow up, I want you to ask yourself whether you are truly expressing your personal brand and honoring theirs, or are you communicating in the expected, standard, "professional way." Some of you may not agree with me on this next point, but if your networking follow-up reads more like a cover letter for a job interview, then you are missing the personal touch.

Getting personal in your follow-up to me looks like this:

1. Send your contacts a birthday card on their birthdays. Better yet, call and sing them "Happy Birthday" on their special day. No matter how bad you think your voice is, the singing telegram is a powerful gift for you to give.

2. Send personalized greeting cards, either handwritten or through an online card sending system.

3. Send a photo of the two of you, which you took during your last meeting. When the person opens your card, e-mail, or letter, he or she instantly smiles seeing a visual memory of a good experience.

4. Your follow-up contains a reference to specific information that you discussed. It's not generic in any way.

5. Use personalized salutations such as "Dear Kathy" and signature closures. I like to use the word "Cheers." I picked up affection for this word while living and working in England for three years. Since having survived ovarian cancer, I find myself using this sign off phrase, "Be well and stay motivated" above my signature and contact details.

6. The voice mail message that you leave has an uplifting vocal quality. Just hearing your voice brings a smile to the person's face.

7. Use the person's name several times when leaving your voice mail message. Everyone likes to hear the sound of his or her own name. Write the person's name a few times in your e-mail correspondence.

8. Personalize any invitation that you send through LinkedIn. Strive to customize each invitation you send by clicking "Connect," followed by "Add a note."

9. End your e-mails and formal letter and cards with a postscript notation. Very few people can resist the power of a P.S. as it draws the eyes instantly.

10. Write your LinkedIn profile summary with a more personalized, conversational tone. Mine starts out, "Thank you for visiting my LinkedIn page to learn more about me. I look forward to connecting with you and getting to know you. I work with_____" (now I get to the meat of my experience, credentials and business focus).

Standout Correspondence

One example of exemplary personalized follow-up that I received was from a woman named Joanna Aversa. She was in the audience of a hundred or so professionals employed by a regional financial institution. I delivered a keynote talk called *Networking Ahead for Your Career* at their annual women's affinity network as part of their diversity and inclusion corporate initiative. During the talk, I shared a simple idea of planting three seeds a day by making phone calls, sending e-mails, texting, and my personal favorite form of follow-up, sending personalized greeting cards, to networking contacts following a meeting.

A few days after the keynote talk, I received the most amazing card in the mail. It was a photo card showing a bunch of carrots freshly picked from a garden. Inside the beautiful card was a handwritten note and a pack of organic carrot seeds. I still have Joanna's card in my office. And course, I immediately called her to thank her. I also e-mailed the leaders at the client organization to tell them how impressed I was with this personalized follow-up in action. A few weeks later, Joanna and I got together for a networking coffee and had the opportunity to get to know each other better. Personalized follow-up works like magic!

Yippee! Who Says You Can't Have Fun with Your Follow-Up?

If something is a drag, you are not going to do it; at least not without putting up a fight or doing a lot of complaining. Whether that something is house cleaning, exercising, or networking follow-up (three things you have to do, by the way), if you don't enjoy it, you won't make time for it, nor will you do it with much gusto.

How do you change something from painful to pleasurable? How do you alter your attitude, so that you enjoy something more than you did in the past?

Part of the solution is that with practice, you get good at it, and, as a result, your confidence and motivation for it will increase. This reminds me of an excellent quote on the subject of motivation from the renowned author, speaker, and leadership guru John C. Maxwell:

"The whole idea of motivation is a trap. Forget motivation. Just do it. Exercise, lose weight, test your blood sugar, or whatever. Do it without motivation. And then, guess what? After you start doing the thing, that's when the motivation comes and makes it easy for you to keep on doing it."

For me, people are fun. Relationships, while sometimes complex and confusing, are rewarding. Why not put a little more fun into how you interact with people in your professional network? Why not laugh a little bit more? Don't take yourself so seriously. Even a job search can be fun if you set your mind to it.

You can approach networking like a game or an experiment. Take a few risks, and measure the results. Read some more books on the subject. Try your hand at a speed networking exercise.

This may be easy for me to say because I have made this my focus, my passion, my expertise. But it wasn't always that way. I had to learn the ropes of networking by doing it and making mistakes along the way. I have been chewed out by a few people who didn't like my approach. It stung at the time, but I moved on. I didn't let them squelch my joy or my results from the very important professional skill of relationship-building.

Fun is a state of mind. You control that; no one else does. The good news is that you can instantly alter your state from moment to moment by thinking different thoughts, conjuring up great memories or making changes to your physiology (i.e., put a smile on your face, laugh, get up and move around). And, of course, the ultimate in fun is hanging around motivated, positive people who are passionate about what they do and can do in the world.

Much of your networking success is in your hands. By having a systematic approach to networking follow-up, you can keep up with an ever-growing network. But if you want to accelerate your networking success or if you need to get a jump start in a new field or region, you may want to insert yourself in established networking groups and professional associations. There are thousands of groups to choose from. In the next chapter, I'll show you why you should consider becoming more involved in your local chamber of commerce.

> *"Whoever said 'the fortune is in the follow-up' first, could have been a billionaire if they only got a penny for every time someone said it. And yet, they've only got it half right. Follow-up is important, that's true. But the real fortune is in the follow-up system."*
> — LISA ROBBIN YOUNG, THE RENAISSANCE MOM

13. Roadside Assistance

Why You Should Join Your Local Chamber of Commerce and Other Networking Groups

If you've ever been stranded on the road because of a flat tire, a mechanical breakdown, or the embarrassing, "I can't believe this happened again, but I locked the keys in the car," you're sure to be grateful for your AAA membership. One phone call and someone comes to rescue you. That's the beauty of roadside assistance—a must-have contingency plan for any driver.

But imagine you didn't have that resource, and you truly were stranded with no one to help you. You might be waiting (or walking) for a long time before help showed up!

For small business owners, roadside assistance is your local chamber of commerce. Big or small, your local chamber is an additional resource on your business team. It will advocate on your behalf with local and state government, it will provide programs to help sharpen your business acumen, it will help to promote your business, and it will give you networking opportunities with other businesses owners, large and small.

The chamber of commerce system in the United States started in 1911 when President William H. Taft set into motion discussions that would launch the U.S. Chamber of Commerce, the world's largest business federation, with more than 3 million businesses across all 50 states. The main purpose of the chamber of commerce system is to promote and defend free enterprise and individual opportunity. With small businesses representing more than three-quarters of all new jobs in the United States, this sector has economic significance. Yet, on their own and without support, small businesses struggle to have their voices heard and to gain access to larger market opportunities as the big boys have. Let's face it; small business budgets are smaller.

But through this channel where enterprising people come together for advocacy, action, and support, their collective voices can be heard. Together, they have greater influence on the economy than they would otherwise have by operating alone.

I belong to one chamber of commerce, and have visited with many more in my role as a professional speaker and program provider. What I enjoy most about chambers of commerce is the accessibility to the executive directors and the relationships you can build with these highly connected leaders. In fact, that is the main job of chambers of commerce—to connect people with opportunity and to support sustained growth of their members.

I have also done my share of griping and complaining that I didn't get much out of my local chamber membership. I ask myself: Why should I send them my money if I don't get the value? Of course, that situation is directly linked to my activity or lack of direct involvement with the chamber. Simply paying your chamber membership is a nice show of local support, but it's not enough to ensure you get personal value from your membership. You must get involved.

Here are 10 ways in which you can get more mileage from your chamber of commerce membership:

1. Personally get to know the executive director of your local chamber of commerce. Have coffee or lunch with him or her. Exchange business cards. Ask how you can be of service to the organization, and ask how it can specifically support you.

2. Satisfy your professional development needs with the chamber's events and programming. Look at their calendar of events, and sign up for seminars, workshops, and discussion groups. Not only will you gain new knowledge and sharpen

your business skills, but also you will meet and mingle with new people.

3. Select an industry forum or discussion group, attend their regular meetings, and/or read their meeting notes. Find out what's going down on the legislative front and how you can work to make positive changes through your chamber. This will help keep you up to speed on industry issues that could affect your business. It could even help to mitigate business taxes. Those who care, take action. Those who don't, just complain.

4. Contribute something of value to the chamber. For example, write an article for the newsletter or website; host a networking event at your place of business; offer yourself or a member of your team as speaker or workshop leader. This platform will naturally spotlight your expertise and your company's capabilities while you are adding to the collective value of the organization.

5. Don't just attend the events, but reach out to your fellow chamber members. Go through the membership roster and identify five to 10 companies and individuals that you'd like to get to know better. Call them and invite them to network with you over coffee. You already have something in common— your chamber membership. This personal outreach effort goes a long way to extending the value of your chamber membership. Don't just show up, but go out of your way to make connections and build relationships with your fellow chamber members.

6. If you make a good connection at a chamber event, remember to follow up and continue the conversation. Don't just collect business cards, but rather, build relationships from within your chamber.

7. Invite others in your network to join your chamber of commerce. Become a friendly recruiter. Your executive director will love you for this, and you will be helping to keep the membership vibrant and interesting. Be sure to make a special effort to introduce your friend/guest to as many chamber members as you know. Help with their orientation whenever you can.

8. Attend the parties and fun events. Who says business can't be fun? When you engage in leisure time with other business people, the relationships usually are enhanced and expedited. Don't be all business all the time. Lighten up and learn to have some fun with your fellow chamber members.

9. Create link love with your chamber of commerce. List your chamber membership on your LinkedIn account and on your company's website, if appropriate. Show your affiliation and commitment to building a strong local economy. Make sure your business listing is current and that your business is appropriately described on the chamber's website. Send your chamber of commerce copies of any press releases that you issue or for events that you are holding. It can help to co-promote you and your business. Why wouldn't you take advantage of these marketing resources? It's part of your membership!

Don't go it alone. Accelerate your professional and business success by joining your local chamber of commerce and getting involved.

10. Get the group discount. If reducing expenses is attractive to you, then you need to learn to leverage your chamber membership and affiliation to get discounts off products and services that you buy locally. Check out the member-to-

member discounts offered by your chamber. The savings you make simply by inquiring could pay for your entire year of chamber membership.

Success by Association

Having a robust professional network means that you have access to more people with influence and connections. You may be fortunate enough to be able to make all the connections and in-roads you need by dealing with people on a one-on-one basis; however, most professionals benefit from participating in different networking groups and professional associations, like your local chamber of commerce. In addition to meeting more people, you have the opportunity to develop yourself professionally with the content, speakers, and resources that chambers offer to their members.

Don't go it alone. Accelerate your professional and business success by joining your local chamber of commerce and getting involved.

> *"When you join an organization, don't wait for your welcome kit to arrive. The kit won't contain any success formula. You create that on your own. To identify your best resource for networking success, just look in the mirror the next chance you get."*
>
> — JEFFREY GITOMER, AUTHOR *THE SALES BIBLE*

Checklist #2

Good job! You've completed Part II of your networking journey. Part III will introduce you to strategies and tactics to help you accelerate your business networking success. When you have completed these actions, you will be ready for Part III.

☐ I am more consciously aware of my body language and the use of my voice and its importance in the networking and communication process.

☐ I have reflected upon my own personal brand and how I want to develop and manage it.

☐ I have developed and practiced my 30-second elevator pitch and am more confident in introducing myself in networking situations.

☐ I have set up a contact management system that stores and organizes all of my networking contacts' information (including e-mail, phone, mailing address, and personal data). It is easily accessible and I can add and update information to it with minimal effort.

☐ I have developed a personalized networking follow-up system that allows me to stay in touch more regularly with my networking contacts.

☐ I have joined and become active in one or more networking groups (e.g., chamber of commerce) and am committed to getting involved with its people and projects in order to maximize my benefits.

PART III

Accelerate Your Success
Overcome Obstacles and Special Situations

14. Turbocharge Your Network

The Networking Funnel of Opportunity

I was teaching a series of networking skills workshops for a client who specialized in accounting and business advisory services. This was part of their in-house programming to help their associates and partners meet the requirements for Continuing Professional Education (CPE) credits. During one of the classes, an astute accountant asked me a very insightful question, "How do you turn a contact into a meaningful connection?"

That got me thinking more deeply about what's involved in actually forming relationships—the kind that can really help you advance your career, business, and life.

I sketched out my initial thoughts on a flip chart right there in the class, but I knew the question deserved more thought. My flip chart drawing was hanging in my office for more than three months. I looked at it repeatedly. I became obsessed with the question, knowing that I needed to outline a clear path that I and others could take to ensure the people we meet in networking situations could grow in importance.

I reflected on the relationships in my own network. I became curious as to how some of them became so meaningful in my life, while others stayed only at superficial levels, or disappeared altogether. What was the magic formula that turned a complete stranger into a lifelong friend?

That's when it hit me. Networking relationships go through a sort of funnel, a leaky funnel. It starts out broad and open, and then begins to narrow and concentrate.

Of course this takes an incredible amount of time, energy, alignment, and good fortune to move from the top of the funnel to the bottom of the funnel. Not every relationship will move through to the end point. Nor should they.

Let me walk you through my thoughts as to how relationships migrate through this metaphorical funnel. This understanding will help you turbo charge your networking and add more power to your career, business, and life.

The Funnel of Networking Opportunity

> *Networking relationships go through a sort of funnel,*
> *a leaky funnel. It starts out broad and open, and*
> *then begins to narrow and concentrate. Not every*
> *relationship will move through to the end point.*
> *Nor should they.*

STAGE #1: STRANGER

We all start out as strangers. People who haven't met. You might have something in common, such as a mutual friend or colleague, the same school or community, or maybe you just come from the same race—the human race. So even though you don't know each other, you don't have to fear strangers. As Will Rogers said, "A stranger is just a friend I haven't met yet."

- **Actions you can take at this stage:** Reach out and introduce yourself. Be civil, polite, and friendly. Don't be creepy and get too familiar too soon. Don't stalk. Allow this stranger to choose to accept your invitation or decline. If you really want to meet them, ask a mutual friend to introduce you.

STAGE #2: CONTACT

You've made contact either online or in-person, but still you don't know a lot about each other. Your brain hasn't yet found a place to file both the face and the name, but if things continue, you might just open up a mental file folder. You might find that you start to run into each other at events and you need to be reminded of their name. For all intents and purposes, they are a number to you. Don't expect too much at this stage. You don't have enough relationship equity to ask for anything...yet.

- **Actions you can take at this stage:** You need to make the effort to get to know them. Spend some time researching their background online. Find out what common connections you have with this person. Where and how do your paths cross?

If you are feeling brave, reach out online or via phone to re-introduce yourself and spend a few minutes to learn more about them. Get their full contact details and send a personalized invitation to connect on the social media network they prefer.

STAGE #3: CONNECTION

By good fortune, you have discovered that you have something in common—perhaps a shared experience, mutual friends, or common goals and beliefs. You can now relate to each other and start to build rapport. You can laugh, smile, and converse more easily with this connection. You start to notice things about them that you appreciate. Their name and face are starting to stick in your short-term memory bank. You enjoy their company and are curious to learn more about them.

- **Actions you can take at this stage:** Make note of your conversation and what they shared with you. Send them a personalized follow-up, noting these items and demonstrating that you paid attention and have a genuine interest in them. If you haven't yet captured their full contact details, do so at this time. Make sure you are connected online and can easily communicate. If this connection is really interesting to you, invite them to have networking tea/coffee or breakfast/lunch with you. Invite them to other networking events that you plan to attend. If you see an article or other resource that you think would interest them, send it. If you promised to make any introductions for them, do so promptly and professionally.

STAGE #4: RELATIONSHIP

Time has passed and you have both invested in this relationship. You have spent quality time together. You know some details of their professional and personal life that they have shared with you. You respect and honor the confidence and trust they have bestowed upon you. You genuinely want to see them succeed and fulfill their goals.

They wish you the best as well. At this stage, you find yourself freely giving and receiving feedback, introductions, guidance, and help. You can easily pick up the phone and speak to them. You might even reach out to them on behalf of another person. You have established relationship equity and you want to protect and nurture it.

- **Actions you can take at this stage:** Stay in regular touch (at least every two months of so). Inquire about their family and the things that are important to them. Don't just talk business. Get personal and show you care. Send them birthday cards. Celebrate their successes. Communicate actively (phone and face-to-face), and passively (social media, e-mail, written correspondence). Make an effort to help them achieve their goals through networking introductions and supporting the causes that they champion. Have breakfast, lunch or dinner with them at least once each year.

STAGE #5: STRATEGIC PARTNER

Your relationship has entered this exciting next stage. You have created enough trust, understanding, and compatibility that it makes sense to align your careers/businesses for mutual growth. Perhaps there is opportunity to refer each other to clients and prospects. Maybe you'd like to evolve this connection into a formal mentoring relationship. Perhaps you might even consider starting a business together or collaborating on new ventures, while maintaining your legal/financial independence. It may be advisable to document your agreements in writing and have an attorney review it. Discuss plainly your vision for how this partnership will work and what processes you will follow.

- **Actions you can take at this stage:** If you sense that there is strategic potential in this relationship, invite the other person to consider formalizing your relationship. You will need to be very transparent and forthcoming with your strategic partner in order to make it work. Regular meetings (in person or virtually) and conversations are essential to maintaining the health of this strategic partnership. Your investment of time, money, and energy will largely determine the success of this partnership.

STAGE #6: LIFELONG FRIEND

It's amazing to reach this pinnacle level of friendship—one that endures the test of time and all trials and tribulations. Friendships are connections that go beyond circumstance and transactions. Friends have your back. They are there for you when you need them and will help you both personally and professionally. They are forthcoming and give you the feedback that other people may be afraid to give you. They have been to your home. You have been to their home. You may have even taken vacations, trips, or outings with these friends. You are comfortable doing business with them, and sharing the more personal aspects of your life. If you asked them, they would drop everything to be there for you. You have done the same for them.

- **Actions you can take at this stage:** Don't take them for granted. This is a significant relationship in your life. Don't let them drift away. Make it a priority to connect regularly with them, and to spend quality time together. Be loyal and faithful to them. If you are in town, make an effort to stop by and visit. Pick up the phone and reach out. Even if you get their voice mail, hearing your voice will make them feel better. Send cards, write letters, share photos, and create memories together. You are there to lift each other up. Encourage, support, and motivate each other!

Put These Ideas into Action

Review your professional and personal networks to determine which people are in each stage of the funnel. Are you happy where they are, or do you think there is more (or less) potential with each person? Realize that you cannot move everyone through this funnel at the same time. You will most surely get a major clog.

Decide which relationships deserve more nurturing—more of your time and attention. Then start applying your relationship building skills at work, at home, and in your community. Your relationships will not only determine how much social capital you have, but also how much happiness and belonging you experience.

The "Networking Funnel of Opportunity" is a reminder of the value that people can bring to our lives. It gives us motivation to move beyond our comfort zones to meet more people. No matter what your current circumstances are, you can create new possibilities for yourself and others by consciously expanding and continuously developing your network.

Time to Accelerate

When I network, I try to remain open to receiving benefits from two seemingly opposing forces: strategy and serendipity. But when it comes to building my business and growing a strong and robust pipeline of future opportunities, I need to put my rainmaker hat on.

In this next chapter I share some of my advanced networking tips and strategies to help you land new business. Even if new business development is not in your job description, you can still learn how to make rain with networking. Your business will love you.

"Relationships, like cars, should undergo regular services to make sure they are still roadworthy."
— ZYGMUNT BAUMAN, POLISH SOCIOLOGIST AND PHILOSOPHER
(1925-2017)

15. Autobahn Ahead

Networking for New Business Development

I remember the very first time I was in Germany and experienced driving on an autobahn. I was the passenger of my German colleague who was driving a gorgeous black Mercedes Benz with cool leather interior. When we merged onto the autobahn and he put his foot on the accelerator, that car just took off. I found myself bracing and going completely silent. My eyes stared at the speedometer as it climbed to 150 kilometers per hour. What was even more startling was when he decelerated to comply with the posted signs once the autobahn stretch had ended. It was like going on a rollercoaster, only not knowing that you were in line to ride.

I later learned that the autobahn, or Bundesautobahn (BAB) as it is officially called, is the federal motorway system that was built in Germany in the 1920's. Switzerland and Austria also have an autobahn system as part of their roadways. The autobahn has no general speed limits. While officials post an advisory speed limit (usually around 130 kilometers per hour or 81 miles per hour), you can go as fast as you feel is safe. Seat belts are required for everyone in the vehicle. There are no speeding tickets or fines for driving too fast on the autobahn; the only risk you take is increasing your insurance liability in the event of an accident.

The Need for Speed

There are times in your life when you need to pick up the speed and get big things done. This is particularly relevant in business development. There are professionals who specialize in this discipline and are well compensated and sought after for their ability to "make rain" and grow the company. Their ability to attract new customers and penetrate new markets makes them highly valuable to any organization. Yet, this skill set can be developed by anyone who wants to grow professional success.

"I want to be a finder, not a grinder." This statement was made by my friend and client, Carol, who is a partner at a successful mid-sized law firm in Connecticut. Carol realized long ago that in order to move up the ranks and increase her compensation, it wasn't enough just to do excellent work and put in long hours. She had to bring in work to the firm. She had to learn how to "make rain" by increasing her competence and confidence in networking and business development. Carol also realized that she needed to teach the other women at the firm how to do the same.

No matter what your field of expertise—law, accounting, technology, or business—your value to the organization will be enhanced if you can master the basics of business development, which includes forming strategic relationships.

Get in the Fast Lane with Strategic Moves

When business development is the goal, your networking strategy needs to be finely tuned. You cannot rely on serendipity or take a casual approach to building your professional network. You need to make strategic moves and build strategic relationships that can take you somewhere significant soon. You must develop an appetite for greater risk and actively push yourself out of your comfort zone. It's time to be bolder and connect to people of greater influence. You have a business to build.

Adopt the Attitude and Behavior of the Rainmaker

The modern definition of a rainmaker is an employee of a company who creates a large amount of unexpected business, consistently brings in money at critical times, or brings in markedly more money than his or her co-workers, thereby "floating their salaries." Every organization needs a few rainmakers on the team.

Personally, I don't think you are born a rainmaker, but rather you can learn the skills and disposition to become one. Following the fundamentals of business development activity, let's take a look at what that might mean in terms of networking:

1. **Assess market opportunity:** Start by thinking about the types of businesses, occupations, and individuals who may benefit from partnering with you on your venture. Drill down into narrower chunks, identifying specific segments within the larger sphere that you think may show greater interest in your value proposition. Write all of this down.

2. **Gather intelligence:** Do your research. Get yourself to your local library and ask the business librarian to show you how to access the numerous databases. Your librarian will know all the best and latest resources for you to use. This is just one of the free benefits of being a card-carrying member of your local library. In addition to the information you can find online, in directories, and in books, research and read articles written by or about your target. Talk to other people in your network who know your potential targets, personally or professionally. Find out where they hang out, and what associations they belong to. Create profiles of the companies and individuals that you identified in step one. Start to prioritize them according to their potential opportunity for you. Once again, write all of this down.

3. **Establish referral partners:** Networking for new business development can be quickly accelerated if you build a highly productive referral partner team of like-minded professionals who serve a similar market. This is particularly useful

networking strategy for anyone in a professional service industry such as accountants, attorneys, bankers, financial advisors, insurance sales, independent consultants, talent development trainers, executive coaches, and professional organizers. Spending time building these referral partner relationships can pay off handsomely over time. It is important to build trust, show appreciation, reciprocate, and have a very clear understanding of what makes a good referral for each of your businesses. In some situations, where legal and appropriate, you might consider setting up a referral partner fee and share in the profits of new business that you gain from the referral. At the very least, I strongly recommend that you express your gratitude with handwritten thank you cards.

4. **Follow up on activity:** Rainmakers are masterful at follow-up. They are organized and disciplined and have a process and system for staying in regular touch. There's no sense in generating leads if you are going to let them languish with poor follow-up. Think about each lead as potentially being worth a million dollars to you. Handle them with extreme care and attention.

5. **Practice your pitch:** When you get serious about business development, you will find that "winging it" is not in your best interest. You've worked too hard to get this far. It's worth your time and effort to practice your pitch and rehearse your presentations. You must be able to articulate your compelling value proposition in a few short minutes. Knowing what you want to communicate and being confident about your ability to deliver it effectively will increase your chances of moving to the next step on your business development timeline. Practice makes perfect; rehearsal primes rain.

6. **Get out there:** Now that you've rehearsed, it's time to get this show on the road. Think about the phrase "location, location, location." You need to be where others gather; know where they go, so that you can meet each other and get to know each other in the networking environment. This is an excellent primer to the future business dealings. If you can make your first encounter outside the normal business office environment, you stand a greater chance to getting an invitation to come in the door. Cold calls are just that—cold. Networking introductions and meeting people in the networking context is a great warm-up to discussing new business opportunities.

7. **Hone your business model:** You have to be very clear about how and where you make money. Who needs your services and who can afford your services are two very different marketing questions. You must learn who your right-fit and wrong-fit clients are. Being very clear on your "who strategy" will help accelerate your networking and business success. When you are rich, your reward can be networking just for the fun of it. Until then, practice strategic networking for business development.

8. **Monitor your progress:** Just like anything you do in business, you must set measurable networking goals and track progress against them. "What gets measured, gets done," my old boss used to say to me. Don't allow yourself to fly by the seat of the pants when it comes to networking. Chart it, graph it, show percent to goal—whatever you need to do to report to yourself how you are doing. If you need help, get an accountability partner, and have that person call you every week and ask you to report on your progress. There's something about having to confess failure to someone else that motivates people to regular action and progress.

9. **Manage your campaign:** As your network grows and you make important new leads and connections, you will want a campaign to stay in regular touch with them. According to Jeffrey Forman, publisher of *The Renegade Network Marketer Review*, "For every month that we don't contact or communicate with our client, we lose 10% of our influence." Mr. Forman lists this on his "scary business facts" page. If this finding is true, I imagine that it wouldn't take long to deplete all that you've worked so hard to build. Your business development success strategy must include a plan to touch base with these important people at least once per quarter. Four times a year will help you stay visible and relevant to them. When opportunity knocks, you want to be near the door to open it.

What's Your Cupcake Strategy?

A few years ago during a coaching session with my business coach Mark LeBlanc, he drew a creative comparison between my business and a cupcake. He explained that my primary service offering— corporate training services—is like the cake in the cupcake; my second best-selling services—executive coaching—is like the frosting (and everyone loves frosting).

The sprinkles, he explained, can turn an ordinary business into something irresistible. They are the little extras that add more value to your core proposition and keep your customers delighted. The sprinkles alone may not be enough to pay the rent, but they add marketing magic to your business.

Then there's the cherry on top of the cupcake—the client attracters. These are the elements of your business and business activity that draw prospects to you, but don't really make a lot of money from it. LeBlanc explained that we can't live on cherries alone; we need to focus on the cake and the frosting to succeed.

I loved this concept so much that I wrote a blog topic on it entitled "What's your cupcake strategy for growing your business?" This article is especially helpful to small business owners and startups, or anyone with an appetite for growing their business.

> *For every month that we don't contact or communicate with our client, we lose 10% of our influence.*

Managing Your Pipeline

Networking is a vital strategy for keeping your future business pipeline healthy. It's not enough to have business today; we must continue to cultivate new prospects and relationships. I remember a major decision I made during the recession of 2008. Several of my major clients had canceled, or put on permanent hold, training engagements that we had agreed to. I was counting on the business and now it was gone. For a moment I had the thought that maybe I should close my business and go out and get a job. But I realized that I had spent a great deal of time and energy cultivating networking relationships and building a strong pipeline. I recommitted to investing in my business through these strategies. I decided that I was going to weather the economic storm. I was in this for the long haul. People still needed my help to grow their careers and businesses perhaps now more than ever. I also decided that I was going to invest more in developing my brand and business so that when the economy improved, I would be in excellent position to take advantage of new opportunities.

Even if you are not a business owner, I want you to take seriously the responsibility of managing your own pipeline of future opportunities. Networking is the art of building and sustaining mutually beneficial relationships *before* you need them. A strong and healthy pipeline that you carefully manage and prioritize will give you more "before" power. It will accelerate your success.

After reading this section, I hope you are more open and curious about the art of new business development. In the next section, we'll take a couple laps around the topic of facilitated networking introductions. Knowing how to do this means you may never have to make a cold call again. Turn the page and let's warm things up.

"Speed matters."

— ERIC MORHAM, RETIRED PRESIDENT OF VINCOR CANADA

16. Never Drive a Cold Car

Warm Up Your Connections with Facilitated Introductions

Cold is not comfortable. Having lived fifteen years in the northeastern part of the United States, I know firsthand it can be pretty miserable to get into your car after a cold, snowy night. The windshield is iced over, the seats are cold, and the engine is not happy. Modern advances such as garages, heated seats, and automatic starters have taken the edge off this problem, but the memory of it reminds me of a problem that most professionals have when it comes to networking and meeting new people: They drive cold.

You've got to warm things up and get more specific about who you want to meet. This is part of a strategy I call "Aim Higher. Get Warmer."

Know What You Want and Where You Want to Go

The first part of this strategy involves the power of specificity. You wouldn't walk into a fancy restaurant and say, "Please give me some food," and expect a fabulous meal that was exactly what you wanted. You may be really hungry, but it helps when you can narrow down the category of what would be appealing to you. This not only helps the wait staff, but helps you to get a better, more satisfying outcome.

One of the wonderful outcomes of networking is that when you build a relationship with others, they are more open to introducing you to people they know. You can help them to help you by being specific in terms of whom you are looking to meet. If they don't know this person, they just might know someone who does. The theory of six degrees of separation suggests that you are within six connections from any person on Earth. That's an amazing, almost unbelievable, concept. Here's an intriguing excerpt from the play, *Six Degrees of Separation* written by John Guare in 1990, which was later made into a movie featuring actors Donald Sutherland and Mary Beth Hurt:

> "I read somewhere that everybody on this planet is separated by only six other people. Six degrees of separation. Between us and everybody else on this planet. The President of the United States. A gondolier in Venice. Fill in the names. I find that a) tremendously comforting that we're so close; and b) like Chinese water torture that we're so close. Because you have to find the right six people to make the connection. It's not just big names. It's anyone. A native in a rain forest. A Tierra del Fuegan. An Eskimo. I am bound to everyone on this planet by a trail of six people. It's a profound thought.... How every person is a new door, opening up into other worlds. Six degrees of separation between me and everyone else on this planet. But to find the right six people."
>
> — MONOLOGUE BY OUISA KITTEREDGE, A CHARACTER IN THE 1990 PLAY *SIX DEGREES OF SEPARATION* WRITTEN BY JOHN GUARE

To tap into this idea, you must be able to articulate whom you are looking to meet. Who in your "future network" have you identified that you'd like to meet and potentially build a relationship with? Be more targeted in your thinking, do your research, and name a living human being who interests you. Know generally why you are motivated to meet that person. Then find a way through your network of being introduced to that person. Ask for a "warm introduction." A warm introduction is when someone introduces you versus making a cold call yourself. A warm introduction will be far easier and more effective than cold-calling or conducting some passive or aggressive marketing campaign. In my book, people always make the best conduits to other people.

{ *Aim higher. Get warmer.* }

A Networking Experiment

A few years ago, I was coaching a corporate rising star; someone identified by his organization as high potential talent with leadership aspirations. As part of my executive coaching program, I was teaching him how to network more effectively and build relationships inside and outside the organization. Most corporate professionals I know (and I was one for 22 years) are usually so buried in their projects that they rarely look up or look around.

When I asked this gentleman who was in his active network, he named about five people he was working closely with in his company. When I asked him who he'd like to add to his future network, he was quiet. He gave me that deer-in-the-headlights look. He couldn't answer the question. He hadn't thought about it—ever. When I pushed him further, he blurted out the name of the CEO of a large Fortune 500 technology company. He was aiming high. I respected that. We discussed how we might make that happen for him, but I'm not sure he was really serious about this goal. He just wanted me off his back for now.

As I was driving home from the coaching session, I reached out and called my friend and former colleague Shirley, who now lives in Southern California. She and I had stayed in touch since we both left a leading direct mail company a few years back. We were both motivated to keep our relationship alive and stay in each other's active network. A call every three months or so seemed to be the glue that our relationship needed to survive the 3,000 mile distance between us.

I casually shared this experience with Shirley, and she surprised me with, "Kathy, you'll never guess who I got an e-mail from yesterday. Our ex-colleague was just appointed to a top executive position at that very company." This intrigued me, but the gentleman who she named was not familiar to me. I had left the company just before he joined. Shirley, however, had worked closely with him and respected him greatly. I smiled, took a deep breath, and popped the question to Shirley.

"Shirley, do you want to participate in a little networking experiment that I am conducting?" I asked in a playful tone of voice. "What do you have in mind?" she asked. "If you will introduce me to this gentleman, then I will ask him if he will meet with my client, who, by the way, is traveling out to attend the company's convention in three weeks. Perhaps they could meet for coffee. Are you game?" I asked her. "Game on," she replied.

Within 24 hours, I received an e-mail from Shirley informing me that she had connected with this gentleman, and he had agreed to do it. "Ball's in your court," her e-mail informed me.

Now for the moment of truth. I had to make a call to a person I didn't know. Not just any person, but a Fortune 500 top executive. I stood up to make the call (a physiology that I find gives me more courage and gumption) and dialed his home number. It was Friday afternoon, and it was now or never. I needed to take the next step in this experiment—for my client's sake and for the lesson.

He answered the phone. I quickly introduced myself and referenced Shirley's referral. I told him about my client and what I was teaching him. I asked him if he would meet my client for coffee when he was at the convention in San Francisco scheduled a few weeks away. He agreed, but on one condition. I listened eagerly. This savvy business leader asked if my client would come prepared to answer a few questions: Why did his company choose them as a vendor? What about times when they chose not to work with them and why not? What other competitors do they use and why? It turns out that my client's organization is a customer of this Fortune 500 business. This "voice of the customer" was an interesting way to get oriented to a new industry and new job. I agreed to these terms on behalf of my client. The experiment had moved to the next stage.

{ *People always make the best conduits to other people.* }

Three weeks later, my client and this top leader met for coffee in San Francisco. It was a good exchange, and my client certainly appreciated the connection and opportunity. I encouraged him to follow up to continue to foster the relationship. Ironically, my client's boss told me later on that he personally knew the CEO of that Fortune 500 Company. As it turns out, my client was only one degree of separation away from his target contact. Funny how that works.

Now's here where the networking magic worked for me. As I reached out to this top executive to thank him for meeting with my client, I asked him if there was anything that I could do for him in return. He e-mailed back to say that he could use some help finding temporary housing in the Palo Alto area and that his wife was looking to join a golf club. Did I know of any good ones in the area? Ironically, this is where I grew up and went to college. And while it had been a while since I lived in the area, I still had strong connections to people who could possibly help with this request.

I immediately jumped into action and accessed my network both professional and personal. Guess who turned out to be the most useful contact for me? My mother. She forwarded my request to my old neighbors, with whom I had lost touch, and friends of the family. Within 36 hours, I had several local area experts giving me "the insider's scoop" on the best places to live and to play golf in the area. I felt empowered to be able to go back to my new networking contact with some specific information and ideas that might help him get settled more easily.

I also reached out via LinkedIn and sent this gentleman an invitation. He accepted it. I read his online profile in depth and looked at the other connections he had listed on LinkedIn. This gentleman had once again proved to me that he was a motivated networker. His behavior, willingness, and online profile demonstrated that he knew how to network and knew the power and importance of relationships.

I like to think this networking experiment was a success on several fronts. I also consider it an ongoing experiment. Time will tell the value of this new connection.

Lending Your Social Capital

Your network has the power of capital—something to invest in that will grow over time. Savvy networkers are willing to lend and borrow social capital often from others whom they know and trust. Of course this comes with some risk, but the rewards are definitely worth considering.

One recent example that comes to mind involved lending my social capital to help a neighbor and friend with her job search. Martha, we'll call her, was a highly skilled technology troubleshooter with deep experience in the insurance industry. She had been laid off when her job was eliminated in a company restructuring. Martha was also shy and reluctant to meet strangers and attend events. Many times I observed her decline, cancel at the last minute, and conveniently get headaches on days involving networking meetings. Her behavior might have suggested that she really didn't want to get another job, and was sabotaging her chances.

"The true value of networking doesn't come from how many people we can meet but rather how many people we can introduce to others."
— SIMON SINEK, AUTHOR OF START WITH WHY

After several attempts of trying to lend Martha my social capital, I decided she needed a hand hold. So I arranged a three-way lunch with a professional friend of mine who was a former board member colleague and corporate leader at a global insurance organization. You might remember her from Chapter 1: Liz. It was the December holiday time and I arranged for a lunch Martha, Liz, and me. We offered to pick up Liz from her office and drive to a nearby Italian restaurant. This extra time in the car to and from the restaurant was a bonus. We brought Liz a small holiday gift to say thank you and happy holidays (not necessary, but nice).

The conversation over lunch was lively and flowed easily. Martha seemed very comfortable with Liz, especially when we got to speaking about gardening in raised beds. Liz showed us photos on her smartphone of the home garden structure that her husband built for her. However, she didn't have a plan on what to plant. This just happened to be one of Martha's personal hobbies, and dare I say, areas of expertise. The two of them went deep on this topic.

As I glanced at my watch, I realized that we were in danger of leaving this lunch without discussing Martha's job search. This would have been a great loss of opportunity, as Liz's company was on Martha's top prospect list. So I made an obvious and necessary pivot, and interrupted the conversation to suggest that we talk business. Both of them seemed relieved. Because so much rapport and "likeability" had been built up in the previous topic, the two of them seemed very willing to help each other. Liz proclaimed "I'll be your (name of her company) Coach. I'll introduce you to key people, help you navigate our system, and scheduled a few 3-way lunches with hiring managers that I know are looking for talented people." This was an incredible offer. I remember thinking inside my head, "I want a (name of her company) Coach, too!" But I held that thought to myself, knowing that this day was about helping Martha, not helping myself. Then the next amazing thing happened. Martha proclaimed, "And I'll be your Garden Coach."

Liz chuckled in delighted. This was not only a wonderful experience, but also, it was a great example of borrowing and lending one's social capital and expertise.

On the ride home I congratulated Martha on a job well done. I coached her on how to take proactive steps in personalized follow-up that would ensure that Liz acted. Martha sent Liz a personal handwritten thank you card with an enclosure of organic garden seeds. I gave her Liz's home address (taking a small risk here), and she mailed this to her home so that it would arrive over the holidays. Liz was delighted when she received it.

Are you curious how the situation with Liz and Martha ended up? Martha entered into negotiations with another insurance company for a potential job. She and Liz agreed that it was sensible to delay facilitating key introductions at Liz's company. I counseled Martha that she should pursue both opportunities at the same time. "It's not over 'til it's over." Liz's offer had been so generous. If nothing else, acting on it would strengthen Martha's networking confidence and broaden her network. It took the other insurance company months to get its act together, but today, as I write this section, Martha is starting her new job. I will encourage Martha to fulfill her offer to be Liz's garden coach. She can still build equity with Liz on a personal front. This connection may be useful in the future for Martha's career, or other people in her network. Building your social capital has long term investment value. By the way, I reached out to Liz today and asked her if she would be my (name of her company) Coach. I also sent her an Easter greeting card to create more warm and fuzzy feelings and to hopefully prompt a return phone call.

> *Your network has the power of capital—something to invest in that will grow over time. Savvy networkers are willing to lend and borrow social capital often from others whom they know and trust.*

Warm It Up

However you decide to do it, I encourage you to make every effort to warm up your networking introductions. You need never make a cold call again. With every introduction you ask for and every connection you help to make for others, you are growing your social capital. It's a powerful skill to master and asset to have. It will create both short-term and long-term value to your career, business, and life.

Next up, we'll explore how you can use social media to ask for and facilitate networking introductions. The advent of social media has unlocked many doors that were previously inaccessible to the ordinary person. That being said, social media has also gotten many people into a lot of trouble. So fasten your seat belts and let's figure out how to leverage social media to positively build your network, as well as your personal brand and professional reputation.

> "The way of the world is meeting people through other people."
>
> — Robert Kerrigan, international business development leader

17. Mind the Gap

Using Social Media to Expand Your
Professional Network

Have you ever used an underground subway system like the one in London? They can be pretty mindboggling. You have to figure out the ticketing system, get comfortable being among a gazillion people, know which of the many tunnels you need to take to get to the right platform, and you must keep your disaster-minded imagination in check. You cannot allow yourself to think of all the terrible things that could go wrong in this bizarre environment. Maybe it's just easier to stay above ground, take a taxi, or walk?

This is not unlike the anxiety that happens the first time you try to master a new social media site. There are so many new ones popping every month that it's hard to keep up. Social media has become a very popular way to make new connections and to stay in touch with people. But there is also the distraction factor. Social media can consume a great deal of your time and energy. If you are not careful, you just might find yourself doing all of your networking online. Some say it all started with the teen-oriented site, myspace, in the summer of 2003. LinkedIn claimed the professional network space in the spring of 2003, quickly followed by Facebook in 2004, and Twitter in 2006. Pinterest launched in 2010, followed by Instagram in 2012. I was frightened when I found an article online entitled "Top 52 Social Media Platforms Every Marketer Should Know." Holy Moly! It's overwhelming. But it's hard to deny that social media has become the new norm for connecting and communicating.

Still I run into professionals (mostly Baby Boomers) who either refuse to play or can't seem to figure it out and remain a novice. This simply cannot stand. We must all stay current with our skills and knowledge. We must force ourselves to learn and adopt new ways in order to stay relevant and in the game. We must do this even if we have to go kicking and screaming.

The title for this chapter, "Mind the Gap," was selected to reflect the normal adoption process of new things. Going below ground is normal for ants and other insects, but not really something human beings are comfortable doing. Once you get the hang of it, it becomes normal and, in fact, is a quite efficient and effective mode of transportation. Perhaps that's why almost every major metropolitan city has an underground transportation system. Even the phrase "mind the gap" has become hugely popular. The phrase was first introduced in 1969 by the London Underground as a warning to alert train passengers of the gap between the train door and the station platform. Some platforms on the Underground are curved, and since the cars are straight, the distance from the platform to the car at certain points is greater, and "mind the gap" is painted in capital letters along the edge of such platforms. I have fond memories of hearing a recorded announcement "mind the gap" which played each time the train arrived. It was followed by "please stand clear of the doors" and "this train is now ready to depart." This familiar phrase and its accompanying logo have become a brand, so popular that it can now be found on T-shirts, coffee mugs, and other novelties. People have figured out how to "mind the gap" safely and to use the underground system to get where they want to go.

And so it is with the social media train. If you have not already gotten on it, you have the opportunity to figure out how to ride this particular transportation system, and utilize it to expand and enhance your professional and personal network. Some of you will learn to use it daily as a valuable system to stay in touch with the important people in your life. Others will use it periodically, but at least you will know how. After all, taxis are pretty expensive, and traffic jams can really slow you down.

Why LinkedIn Is a Great First Step

LinkedIn is perhaps the easiest of the social media sites to figure out and maintain. It is also the "safest" in terms of managing your professional image. You are allowed to post one profile photo. I strongly recommend that you upload a professional headshot, in order to help distinguish you from the many other people in the world with your same name. According to the company, LinkedIn has more than 467 million registered members in more than 200 countries (as of April 2017). Of those registered members, more than 106 million members are active (according to Wikipedia). LinkedIn is available in 24 languages. The company website claims that two new members join LinkedIn every second, and that students and college graduates are its fastest growing demographic. As a sign of its success and promise, the Microsoft Corporation purchased LinkedIn in 2016 for $26 billion.

Everybody's Doing It

Of course, these LinkedIn numbers pale by comparison to the users of Facebook (FB). Reports estimate that there are more than 1.86 billion active users who have logged into FB in the past thirty days. Founder, chairman, and CEO of Facebook, Mark Zuckerburg ranked number six of the World's Top 10 Billionaires in the Forbes 2016 report, with a net worth of $44.6 billion. Not bad for a 31-year-old leader.

Twitter is in third place, with 319 million monthly active users using this microblogging site (as of April 2017). With the Twitter addiction Donald Trump has demonstrated during the first 100 days of his U.S. Presidency, this social media site is getting a great deal more buzz. I wouldn't be surprised if the Twitter user base, market valuation, and popularity increase rapidly over the next few years as a result of this presidential exposure. It's amazing how much conversation can be stirred up in just 140 characters.

Time Management Tips for Using Social Media

Social media, like e-mail, can become habit-forming. You get involved in it, and before you know it, you have spent several hours "getting nothing important done." As with all things electronic (TV, phone, Internet, texting, social media), you must put some parameters around it in order to safeguard your time.

Here's what I do: I treat social media like my daily vitamin. I have a specific time in which I take it, and I check in with it at least once a day. I don't take more than I need, and I don't sit there for hours studying the bottle. Continuing with this metaphor, I try to get most of my nutrients the old-fashioned way: by eating well and living a healthy lifestyle. In networking terms, that means spending quality time with people, face-to-face. Social media should be used to supplement and reinforce your in-person efforts, not replace them. So use social media responsibly, and don't completely substitute quality of contact for efficiency of texting, tweeting and the like.

How to Expand Your Network Using Social Media

The first place to start is by inviting the people you already know to join you on the social media site of your choosing. Search to see if they are already there, send them an invitation, "follow" them or "friend" them (depending upon the vernacular of your selected social media site). Check out who they know and with whom they are connected. Invite those people to join you. If you see someone that you don't yet know, but who looks interesting to you, request that your friend introduce you through the electronic functionality of the social media site.

> *Use social media responsibly, and don't completely substitute quality of contact for efficiency of texting, tweeting, and the like.*

When reaching out to connect with people online, do your best to personalize the invitation. Mass standard communication is out; custom personalization is in. You need to make sure that you are not being generic in your communication. While social media can help you connect in the digital age, you still need to make an effort to personalize it. Please don't be one of those people who hit the "lazy" button on social media. Take 30 seconds to write a few short sentences expressing why you wish to connect on line with them.

If you are using LinkedIn, be sure to create a complete online profile, listing every school you have attended, every place you have worked, and every community group with which you are involved. This will tell the technology smarts behind the system to send you suggested contacts. This is a great way to reconnect with people you may have lost touch with or forgotten about. It's easy to renew connections of the past through these social media sites. It's the modern memory aid.

If you are of the mind to expand your network strategically and make specific new connections, you can mine your friends' contact lists. That is, once you are linked in with them at the first level, you can look at their contacts, which will show you your shared contacts (the people you are both connected to) and the other connections. You may find someone you know just as I did seconds ago while perusing LinkedIn. You can send that individual an invitation to connect with you using this vehicle. A few of these per week, and your online network will grow rapidly. If you have LinkedIn's premium InMail subscription, you have even more latitude to get connected to influential people you find on this platform.

> *When reaching out to connect online, do your best to personalize the invitation. Mass standard communication is out; custom personalization is in.*

Now that You Have These Connections, What Do You Do with Them?

It's not enough just to amass a huge contact list (the numbers game); you have to activate the lines of communication. Casual acquaintances are nice, but meaningful relationships are more powerful. To achieve this online, you must do a couple of things on an ongoing basis.

1. **Let your contacts know that you are still alive by posting a meaningful update at least once per week.** By meaningful, I mean that you share with them what you are working on, what's coming up in your world, or what new things you have discovered. Resist the urge to post trivial updates or compromising photos of yourself or others. Instead, look at your week, past or present, and share something noteworthy. It could be an accomplishment, a helpful resource, or a combination of the two, such as "I just finished facilitating a one-day workshop on building your personal leadership brand. Check out this helpful resource on the topic." (Be sure to include the link).

2. **Share your latest affiliations and achievements.** You can do this by adding something to your profile, which will be shared automatically with your contact list. You might just get a few "congratulations" back, which is an opportunity to catch up in conversation online or offline.

3. **Engage others in conversation.** Ask for their opinions. For example: "My company is trying to put guidelines around social media usage for employees. Does anyone have any resources or suggestions?" or "I'm going to write a blog post on confidence killers. I'm curious what zaps your confidence and what you do to get back on the horse."

4. **Comment on their posts.** Scroll through their updates, and if one catches your eye, comment on it. This tells your contacts

that you are paying attention and that you care about them. This touch point counts toward building a stronger relationship with them.

5. **Post a quote slide periodically on your social media site.** People love to look at pictures and read inspiring quotes. You can find readymade quote slides on BrainyQuote.com or Pinterest. You can also create your own quote slides by using your own photos or buying stock photography (such as istockphoto.com). Then find your favorite quote online. Be sure to double check the source of the quote as you want to get that right. You can even quote yourself. There are many graphic design software programs that are easy to use. I find myself often defaulting to PowerPoint software, where I can insert the photo image, layout the text the way I think looks best, and then save the image as a jpeg file. It's not the best program, and quite frankly it requires too many steps, but I have figured it out and I know what to do. One other tip is to create your own repository of your favorite quotes and visual quote slides. They are wonderful to use on social media and in presentations. Heck, you can even create your printed greeting cards with these quote slide images.

How Can You Maintain Your Relationships Using Social Media?

One of the biggest drawbacks of social media is inactivity. People notice this. You may have an account, but if you don't respond for months, it becomes very obvious and could alienate people in your community. It's a little like launching a website for your business and never once updating it—nice online brochure, but not very engaging. Google will frown upon you, as will your visitors.

Regular usage is important, so you need to figure out how to include this in your daily or weekly routine. For some of you, this may require overcoming your fear of the technology monster and forcing yourself to learn a few new tricks. Don't allow yourself to become a dinosaur by making excuses like: "I don't have time to waste with that social media stuff," or "I don't like the computer that much," or "I don't want my private information out there for strangers to probe." This fear-based reluctance will only hold you back. Remember that when you were very young, you learned to stand and walk all by yourself. If you could do that as an infant, you can certainly learn how to use social media to your advantage. We are learning machines!

The Importance of Managing Your Digital Presence

When I am working with professionals under 30, I often have to remind them of the critical importance of managing their online personas with care. Everything matters. If you think future employers aren't going to check out your social media as part of their hiring due diligence, think again. The photos, the comments, even your "nickname" or e-mail account name speak volumes about you. And these records are permanent. Don't be naïve enough to think that these images and correspondence won't be noticed by people whose decision-making powers will affect your future. When in doubt, don't post it. Everything matters online. It's part of how you communicate your professional image and express your personal leadership brand.

One common problem is that people forget their passwords and can't get back on line to update their social media sites. I also run into professionals who for some reason end up with two or more profiles on the same social media platform. This dilutes their digital presence, confuses people, splits up their network, and makes them look less than savvy. If you are in this situation, please resolve it immediately by studying the FAQ (frequently asked questions) that is provided by the social media platform in question. Follow their step-by-step instructions or hire a social media professional to eliminate the duplicated profile. Allowing this problem to continue for months and years on end is so unnecessary, and dare I say unprofessional.

> *Everything matters. If you think future employers aren't going to check out your social media as part of their hiring due diligence, think again.*

LinkedIn Is Not a Dating Site

Your online behavior also matters. Nothing creeps me out more than when I accept an invitation from someone I don't know (but they are a friend of a friend), and the next thing I know they are sending me inappropriate messages that they find me attractive and want to get to know me better. This is especially disturbing when it's on LinkedIn. I once accepted an invitation from a veterinarian based out of Philadelphia. He had a professional photograph, a well-written summary and background. I was shocked when he wrote me a four paragraph love-letter on LinkedIn. I felt violated and immediately blocked him from my account. I wrote a blog post called "Social Media Creep Factor" (August 10, 2016) and provided actions and options for recourse and protection. I suppose it is easy online to pretend that you are someone that you are not and prey on people. Personally, I find it totally unacceptable and unprofessional. Please remember that LinkedIn is not a dating site.

Social Media Etiquette

Can your social media activity get you fired from your job? Can it stop you from getting the job you want? We've all heard stories about this. And the answer is yes, it can do both of these harmful things to your career. So it is imperative that you practice social media etiquette. When in doubt, don't tweet. Unsure? Read your company's social media policy. Feeling risky? Take a break and consider the negative consequences before you post the photo or negative comment on social media.

For advice, I often turn to Barbara Pachter. She is an internationally renowned business etiquette and communications speaker, coach, and author. I met Barbara at the Greater Women's Hartford Conference where we were both teaching workshops. As Barbara was flying in for this conference, I thought I'd reach out, introduce myself, and offer to give her a lift back to the airport after the conference. (See the rideshare networking tip in the "Fuel Extenders" Chapter 27). She accepted and that began our professional connection.

When Barbara notified me that she was publishing her tenth book entitled *The Essentials of Business Etiquette: How to GREET, EAT, and TWEET Your Way to Success* I just had to order it. In her book, she provides insight into how social media can provide business opportunities for you, as well as get you into trouble. Below are some of the sensible tips that I gleaned on how to conduct myself on social media with good business etiquette:

- **Provide value.** Have a strategy for your postings. Link them to your business focus and area of expertise. Let people know what professional meetings you are attending, so that they are in the know about networking meetings and opportunities.

- **Know what your customers and clients are doing.** This knowledge can help you establish relationships with them.

- **Avoid criticizing your employer.** And for that matter, don't disparage your peers, clients, or even competition. Negative commentary casts a dark shadow on you, rather than the person or thing you are complaining about on social media.

- **Don't put people down, curse, or make racist statements.** Not only is this rude, mean-spirited, and unprofessional, it could cost you your job and/or opportunities. This tip applies to both online behavior as well as off-line.

- **Never post offensive photos or videos on any social media site.** What you put on social media is public and permanent. When you post comments that are hateful, insulting, rude, or nasty, not only can you hurt someone, you can put yourself in harm's way, both professionally and legally.

- **Control your privacy settings.** Learn the privacy options available to you for each social media platform you engage with. Select them carefully. And always remember that what you post (even to a small private group) can potentially be shared with their networks on social media.

When in doubt, don't post it. Take a walk, cool down, and get back to your happy place. Now you are ready to do productive online networking.

Staying Relevant

For those who are "older", it can be frightening to think that the younger generations have grown up in a whole different world. They have no memory or experience with typewriters. They don't learn typing skills; they have keyboarding skills. They are less likely to have traditional phone lines, and are more likely to conduct their lives online with their mobile communication devices. In many ways, they can move, think, process, and adapt much faster than older folks. They don't fear technology; they hunger for the next great app.

So how do you keep up with them? You can't just write it off as a passing phase or condemn it; you must get on board, or else you risk becoming irrelevant. These young professionals will be your future customers, your future bosses, and your future caretakers. You must seek to understand, appreciate, and communicate with them their way.

What's the solution? Work with them. Hire them to help you get with the new program. Have your daughters or sons show you how to work the social media sites. Let them be your guides into the new way of doing things. By teaming with them, you will not only get your skills and online profiles up to date, but you also will be building a powerful new bridge with our future leaders. They too are important to add to your professional network.

And if you are "younger" and have grown up with the internet and social media, you will need to work on your personal communication skills. You need to feel as comfortable and confident connecting in person and over the phone as you do online. This will require you to get out and go to events and strengthen your rapport building muscles. Discipline yourself to "power down" during face-to-face meetings and events so that you can be fully present. Work on your handshake and eye connection. Practice standing and sitting "in stature." This nonverbal body language communicates a great deal about who you are and what you are capable of. It sends silent signals that will either attract people to you or repel people from you. I encourage you to cultivate these "soft skills" and use them to present your professional best at all times.

The next topic we'll explore is differences in how men and women network, and how you can be more nimble and comfortable no matter which gender you are connecting with.

> *"Social media is changing the way we communicate and the way we are perceived, both positively and negatively. Every time you post a photo, or update your status, you are contributing to your own digital footprint and personal brand."*
>
> — Amy Jo Martin, author of *Renegades Write the Rules* and host of *Why Not Now?* podcast

18. Who Is the Better Driver?

How Men and Women Network Differently

"This car doesn't go very fast," was my casual complaint to my husband some years ago when I was driving a red convertible Miata. Those were the days, before kids and before I realized that skin cancer can result from too much top-down driving. I had the most incredible commute to my job at Southcorp Wines of Australia where I served as marketing manager of the hugely successful Lindemans brand, including the flagship Bin 65 Chardonnay. The office was in Monterey, California, which meant I got to drive along the absolutely gorgeous coastline of Highway 101—in a red convertible, no less. The awakening came when Byron, my husband, got behind the wheel of the Miata. I had no idea that little car could go so fast. I was gripping every handle that I could find inside the passenger cabin, just to protect myself. With a blood-drained white face and wide-eyed stare, I looked at him, and he said, "This thing will go fast; you just need to know how to drive it."

I'm not sure what the national statistics on speeding and driving records are for men and women in the United States, but in my household, there is a notable difference in driving styles and speed. The same can be said for our different approaches to building relationships.

Do Men and Women Network Differently?

Of course men and women network differently. We think differently, we communicate differently, and we relate differently. Even our brains work differently, according to developmental molecular biologist Dr. John Medina, who wrote the book *Brain Rules: 12 Principles for Surviving and Thriving at Work, Home and School.* Scientists have discovered differences between men's and women's brains in the front and prefrontal cortex, areas of the brain that control much of the decision-making ability. They have found differences in the limbic system, which controls our emotional life and mediates some types of learning. And lastly, they have uncovered prominent differences in the amygdala, which impacts emotions and our ability to remember.

Conversation versus Commotion: Different Ways to Cement a Relationship

Dr. John Medina goes on to cite the work of behaviorist and author Deborah Tannen, who has studied gender differences in verbal capability among other things. One of my favorite books by Tannen is *You Just Don't Understand: Women and Men in Conversation*. She gives insight into the gender differences in how men and women go about cementing relationships. These differences can be seen early on between how boys and girls play as evidenced by the following clinical observation:

> "When girl best friends communicate with each other, they lean in, maintain eye contact, and do a lot of talking. They use their sophisticated verbal talents to cement relationships. Boys never do this. They rarely face each other directly, preferring either parallel or oblique angles. They make little eye contact, their gaze always casting about the room. Instead, commotion seems to the central currency of a little boy's social economy. Doing things physically together is the glue that holds their relationship intact."

Perhaps this doesn't surprise you. But think about it in terms of professional networking. Men tend to golf while women meet for coffee and conversation. I know that this is a huge generalization and ignores individual differences in style and preferences, but I think it sheds light on some of the fundamental differences in how certain men and women network differently. The good news is that neither one is right or wrong, neither one is better or worse. They just are two different approaches. They both can work.

Does This Stuff Work Better for Women?

Occasionally during my workshops on networking skill development, a man will ask me if my networking methods and techniques are more effective with women. This question has stopped me a few times and given me reason to pause and consider if my methodology is an outgrowth of my own personal preferences. Of course it is. But I have balanced that viewpoint by working with many male clients and networking colleagues over the years. Our approaches to networking may be different in some ways, but the belief in the importance of relationships to business and career success is fundamentally the same.

Spending Quality Time with People of Influence

It has been my observation that women tend to build relationships through conversation, while men tend to build relationships through activity. Perhaps that's one of the reasons why golf remains one of the most compelling "venues" for men to network and build business relationships.

There is power in the game of golf, notably the opportunity to spend quality time with people of influence. It is the quintessential business networking activity, at least for the Baby Boomers. The jury is out on how Millennials will network. Can you golf and text at the same time?

Men have been leveraging the golfing "venue" for networking and relationship-building forever, it seems. Women are catching on to this opportunity. More and more women are starting to take lessons and are getting more comfortable playing golf and conducting business on the golf course. I suppose it's a new spin on equal opportunity—equal play for equal day's work.

Time Crunch

However, for many professional women, the idea of taking four hours out of the workday to spend leisure time with other business people is simply out of the question, even if their male colleagues do it as a regular course of business. Are women too responsible or too shortsighted to see what we are missing? Perhaps women need to look at this situation through a different lens. We might, therefore, consider the idea that business doesn't always have to be conducted in an office or traditional "place of business." Building and sustaining your professional relationships through sport and other enjoyable activities just might create the networking magic you need to accelerate your career and business growth.

What if You Don't Like Playing Golf?

Well, there's always food; you can network over lunch, dinner and/or morning coffee. You can go for a walk and get some fresh air (just try not to get too winded as that looks bad for business health.) Doing things together is an excellent way to enhance the relationship, as long as you are focused on the relationship as much as you are on the activity. Remember that your sportsmanship and conduct in that activity will say a lot about your character and professionalism in other contexts such as business. Don't get carried away in the winning/losing aspect of the activity. It's being together that matters in networking.

> *Building and sustaining your professional relationships through sport and other enjoyable activities just might create the networking magic you need to accelerate your career and business growth.*

Let's Get Together for a Manicure

What other venues are available to you to conduct networking and relationship development? How about meeting for a manicure and conversation? Could you actually rationalize that in your own business mind? How about the guys?

I had a client who worked for a CPA firm. She had attempted once to get a client entertainment expense preapproved by her (male) partners for an outing to a day spa with her best client. The partners balked at the idea and declined her request. One hour later, they were headed for the golf course to conduct business with their best client.

What's the Difference?

Manicure with clients versus a round of golf with clients? Time spent in any leisure activity creates an opportunity to discuss business in a more open, relaxed environment. The venue and activity may be different, but the goal is the same: strengthening the professional relationship.

Whatever Floats Your Boat

My networking friend Jane shared her thoughts on the question of golf versus manicure. She said it was a matter of appreciation and motivation: "Whatever floats your boat. If they like it, do it together." In my opinion, Jane is a master connector and relationship-builder extraordinaire. Through the years, she has spent time with clients and networking contacts in all sorts of venues and activities, including salons, golf courses, restaurants, and going for walks in nature. It's not the venue or the action that makes the difference, it's the togetherness.

Have More Fun in Your Networking

Do men and women network differently? Thank goodness we do. We have much to learn from each other if we open our minds and appreciate our differences. Your professional network should include both men and women and people from all walks of life. Consider it a balanced portfolio. Make it a priority to build and sustain these mutually beneficial relationships with all sorts of people. Take time to find out what they enjoy doing. Ask, "What kinds of hobbies or activities do you enjoy?" Find out what energizes them. If you have common interests, consider the possibility of spending time together in this activity. Why not have a little fun along the way of building your professional network?

There's a great deal of joy and fun to be had when networking with others. But there are also the frustrating times—especially when you run into roadblocks. The next chapter will give you tips and ideas on how to get around these barriers and continue driving toward networking success.

> *"The biggest mistake is believing there is one right way to listen, to talk, to have a conversation or a relationship."*
>
> — Deborah Tannen, American author, academic and professor of linguistics at Georgetown University in Washington, D.C

19. Speed Bumps

How to Network Around Barriers

Not everyone moves at the same speed. Some people will get frustrated with you if you go too slowly, while others will get annoyed if you move too fast. When you are on "their turf," sometimes people will put up invisible speed bumps to deliberately slow you down. Rather than just plowing through these relationship barriers and potentially damaging yourself, let's explore some finessed ways in which you can cooperate with the barriers and still get what you want out of the professional networking process.

Befriending the Gatekeeper

Many of the influential people you will want to connect with will be surrounded by a small army of gatekeepers—protecting them and coordinating their every move. Many people develop a dislike for these gatekeepers, mostly because they can't seem to get through them or around them to get to the decision maker. I think this attitude is at the very root of the problem. If you've ever been an administrative assistant or known one, you are aware that for the most part, people treat administrative assistants like the low man on the totem pole. They don't often get the respect or recognition they deserve. Many clumsy networkers and sales professionals view these administrators as faceless, valueless voices. This is a big mistake. Why? Because these administrators have tremendous influence and knowledge of the very person with whom you are trying to connect. Finesse move number one is to take the time to get to know the administrative assistant. Know his or her name, and find out and remember what matters to them. Program that person's number in your cell phone and add the individual to your professional network. Ask how you can help. Treat the administrator as a valuable person, and take the time to build a relationship with her or him. Then your gatekeeper will likely give you an Easy Pass to the decision-maker. But you must earn that pass through respect and common courtesy.

Not Enough Time

Every working professional faces one major foe—the time demon. We never have enough of it, and there are many demands on it. It feels like the clock and calendar run us versus the other way around. And while we might want to spend more time with things like networking and with people and learning, the reality is there's just not enough time in the day.

If you run into time as a speed bump, don't take it personally and don't fight it. It will win every time. You must learn to outsmart time. "Be lazy like a fox" is one of the chapter headings from the book *Womenomics* by Katty Kay and Claire Shipman. The idea is that you must learn to work smarter, not harder or longer. The authors suggest that we put limits on our schedules and announce our "think time." They suggest that you even broadcast a rule that unless it's urgent, you'll be answering e-mails and phone calls in the mornings and late evenings. The authors also recommend to "mind your meetings" which means reducing the amount of time wasted in unproductive meetings. If the meeting is not necessary or your presence is not essential (meaning that it's critical to the decision-making process), then graciously decline the meeting and ask to be informed of the outcome. We must learn to say "No." If it feels better, say "No, thank you."

Now, if you are on the other end of the "No, thank you" time demon management strategies, there are a few things you can do to support this effort:

1. Leave short, succinct voice mail messages with your contact information and a compelling reason to call you back. No more long-winded, cut off messages. Don't waste their time or you'll kill your opportunity.

2. Learn to get to the point quickly and put the good stuff upfront. Know ahead of time what you want to ask, and be ready with options. Learn to be comfortable thinking on your feet (and on the phone).

3. Meet on the move. Offer to drive the person or go with him or her to meetings or an event. Time in the car together can be like gold for the relationship. You are doing a service for that person and having exclusive time together.

4. Offer to bring lunch to that individual. Many executives and business owners are working and eating on the run, but they have to eat sometime. Offer to bring sandwiches or coffee to their office and chat over a meal or beverage together. Food is magic!

5. Schedule networking meetings in shorter time increments, and mind the clock. Rather than asking for the traditional 30 or 60 minute meeting, request 15 or 20 minutes. Or be like my business coach Mark LeBlanc who often says, "When you can find 17 minutes, let's jump on the phone and discuss it." Don't chit chat, dialogue, or tell them your whole life story. Discipline yourself to be more focused and concise when networking. This will demonstrate your professionalism and your consideration and respect for their time.

6. If you can get it done on the phone, do it. Don't demand face time if the person doesn't have time to give. You can build rapport and relationships on the phone quite effectively. I find it's a better medium than e-mail or even social media, because

they experience more of you when they hear your voice. When the time is right, you can meet in person, break bread together, and deepen your connection and appreciation for each other.

{ *Your first job in the networking encounter, whether by phone, e-mail or face to face, is to put the other person at ease. It's called rapport-building.* }

Dealing with Skepticism

Many people are suspicious of people who "want to network" with them. They fear that this is a mask for wanting to sell something or ask for a job. If you are in business for yourself, many people will treat you like a "vendor" and keep you at arm's length. Your job as a savvy networker is to put the other person at ease with you quickly. This is most likely going to happen on the phone, so sprucing up your phone skills and confidence is important to your networking success. Learn how to mirror and match different vocal patterns. If the other person speaks quickly, you should speak quickly; if he or she speaks slowly, you must slow down too.

You may find that having someone else pave the way for your first meeting or call helps to break the ice. This can be done through an e-mail introduction or even using social media. You might find it useful to let the person know that you'll be calling them to introduce yourself. Be pleasant and friendly, but don't waste his or her time. State your intention, and suggest a time and date when he or she might be available to meet with you in person. Here's a sample phone conversation:

"Hello Margery. My name is Kathy McAfee, and we have a mutual friend in Richard Meta. (Pause for recognition.) Richard has strongly recommended that we connect and do a little networking together. I thought I'd take the initiative and reach out and introduce myself to you. Do you have time to talk now, or would you prefer to schedule some time next week when perhaps we could meet for coffee? I have time on Tuesday morning, if that works for your schedule."

Your first job in the networking encounter, whether by phone, e-mail or face to face, is to put the other person at ease. It's called rapport-building, and this is a learnable skill that will greatly enhance your networking success (more about rapport-building in Chapter 8).

The Budget Objection

You may find yourself running up against the budget objection. "I can't afford that right now," or "We don't have the budget now; therefore there's no reason for us to meet." If this happens to you, remind the person that your intention is not to sell anything but rather to connect and see if you can help each other in any way. There are tons of ways to create value in networking that don't involve money. There is great long-term value in creating mutually beneficial relationships before you need them. Disarm the person with a surprising statement like:

"That's okay because I have nothing to sell you. I just wanted to introduce myself and have the opportunity to get to know you and for you to get to know me. I imagine that we could both help each other in some way. That's the beauty of networking. What's open on your calendar next week?"

The Black Hole of Non-Response

This is perhaps the toughest rejection of all. Your e-mails don't get opened, your calls don't get returned, your letters go unanswered. Don't take it personally; people are just busy and can't keep up with the inundation of correspondence. They are willing to sacrifice a little civility just to survive their day. If you are not their boss, their spouse, their child, their client, or their parole officer, they don't have to return your call. What do you do about this situation? You get creative, and you get kind. Find a way to touch base that makes the person smile and brings joy or relief to his or her day. This is where sending personalized greeting cards or small gifts can bring life to their day. Low-cost items, such as food, garden seeds, flowers cut from your garden, travel books, family photos or funny movies from your collection, can make all the difference in the world. These small acts of kindness can be huge door-openers. Be careful not to junk up their e-mail inbox with jokes, cartoons, and e-cards that take more time to process and delete. This doesn't bring relief; this creates burden. If you want response, then find ways to be more engaging.

Patience is a Virtue

We all remember the lesson provided in "The Tortoise and the Hare" fable attributed to Aesop. Sometimes the more methodical and patient person wins out over the fast, arrogant, and careless one. A little patience and finesse go a long way in networking and relationship-building. Slow and steady combined with caring and confident wins the race in the long run.

Speaking of networking finesse, have you ever had an awkward moment ending a conversation at a networking event? I certainly have. So I have developed strategies to confidently exit situations and politely end conversations without looking or feeling like a jerk. Keep reading because this next section will be very useful to you.

> "Good friends are like shock absorbers. They help you take the lumps and bumps on the road of life."
> — FRANK TYGER, EDITORIAL CARTOONIST (1929-2011)

20. One-Way Roads and Exits

*How to Gracefully End Conversations
and Move On*

One-way roads have always been a bit tricky for me. Some cities are full of them, and if you don't know the landscape, you can get really messed up. There are some people who just have an innate sense of which is the right way to go and when to exit. One such person is my nephew, Adam. When he was only five years old, I took him to the Tech Museum of Innovation in San Jose, California. I had just moved back after working and living in England for three years. I had to re-adjust to driving on the right side of the road. After a fun-filled day, Adam and I returned to the car; I buckled him in his safety seat in the back and got myself into the driver's seat. I could see his cute little face in the rear-view mirror. As I began to exit the parking area, I was momentarily confused as to which way I should turn. The road was unfamiliar to me. I decided to turn right. From the back of the car, a little voice spoke out, "You're going the wrong way." It was eerie that such a young child would know which way to turn, but he was correct. I was about to drive down the wrong direction on a one-way street. Disaster averted thanks to the GPS instincts of a five-year-old boy.

Zero to 60: Take Your Time in Networking

Going the wrong way in networking happens all too frequently. It can happen when you are being too pushy or aggressive; forcing a relationship to advance faster than the other person is comfortable with or ready for. This doesn't work in the romantic dating world, nor does it work in professional networking. You must give the budding new relationship some breathing space. The key here is patience and appropriate levels of follow-up.

Keep Your Eyes on the Road (Not the Visor Mirror)

Another one-way road that is overused in networking is the "I-message"—talking too much about yourself and dominating the conversation. You can come off as arrogant and self-absorbed to other people, or perhaps even nervous. Since I grew up with the nickname "Chatty Kathy," you can imagine that I suffer from this one-way lure.

Sometimes you have to experience someone else making the mistake before you can recognize it in yourself. I call this the buffet-moment. Here's one such time in my networking experience:

I attended a women's networking event as a guest of a former client of mine. I am still friendly with many of the women from that firm. The featured activity was speed networking—a cross between speed dating and networking. In this setup, we sat in round tables of eight women. We each had two minutes to introduce ourselves; the bell would ring when the time was up, and then the next person would have the floor. We went through three table rounds of this exercise. It was excellent practice and a good way to meet more of the women in the room.

When I moved to the third table, one woman—let's call her Mia—took charge immediately. She changed the rules and told us that we had to share something about our personal life. The vocal power and body language that she exhibited in her opening presentation sent a clear signal that she was bossy by nature. Rather than leading by example, she instructed the woman to her left to begin immediately. She opted to go last (nice leadership move, Mia). When it came around to her turn to speak, I was shocked to see that she broke her own rules. She bragged (and I do mean bragged) about her many professional accomplishments. She spoke nothing of her personal life until the very end, when she boasted that she was married to a military officer who was a gourmet cook. Once again, the tone of her voice and her gestures stripped away any humility in her delivery.

While she spoke, I noticed she started nearly every sentence with the word "I."

- I do…
- I choose only to work with…
- I am married to…
- I am certified in…
- I am expert in…
- I drive…
- I work for…
- I am…
- I…

Mama Mia! That's more than anyone can handle.

Now the I-message is a powerful interpersonal communication tool. It allows you to take ownership of your feelings and experiences and to express yourself without casting blame or triggering other people. But when you use too much I-messaging in the context of networking, you project the image of being too self-absorbed and too focused on self. You lose out on the opportunity to create relevance and to relate with the people with whom you are networking.

I drove home from the event reminding myself to keep my eyes on the road and to keep my own I-messages in check. After all, the purpose of networking is relationship-building, not the glorification of I.

Pay Attention to Other Drivers

One way to avoid the problem of too much I-message is to learn to listen and ask more questions. Make it your goal to learn something new every time you meet with people. Learn to retain that knowledge in your short-term memory. Don't allow it to escape instantly (in one ear and out the other), but make sure you hold on to at least some of it through active listening. I love to preface my questions with the phrase "I'm curious about…" If you can get the other people to open up and talk about themselves, then you are going to be credited for being a great conversationalist.

You might want to practice what my friend Marge calls "the art of being in service of others." Be "others-centric," rather than "me-centric," and make it your first priority to get to know the other person. This takes all the pressure off you to give your elevator pitch or your 30-second commercial. Marge suggests starting with open-ended questions such as, *"Tell me about yourself."* Notice how different that feels from the more direct work-related question that everyone expects to hear and hates: "What do you do for a living?" Marge's question allows people to share more about themselves than just their job, which may not be their passion. It's hard not to like someone who expresses genuine interest in learning more about you.

Which Exit to Take?

Perhaps the most stressful moment in networking is the awkwardness of not knowing how to gracefully leave a conversation. You don't want to get stuck with the same person all evening. Quality is important, but in networking, you need to pay attention to the quantity of connections as well. Sometimes you find yourself clinging to certain people out of fear of meeting new people. Other times, people cling to you. If neither party is skilled or confident in graceful exits, it could turn a nice connection into a long, dull, and boring one. In networking, you must learn how to exit and move on to new roads.

{ *It's hard not to like someone who expresses genuine interest in learning more about you.* }

There is an art to the graceful, confident, and natural exit, where people can end their conversation and move on to meet other people without feeling weird about it. This you need to practice and get good at. You'll need to do it to be successful in networking. You must learn not only to say "hello," but also to say "goodbye, see you later."

Here are a few tips on how to get good at the exit.

1. **Be direct.** "I think it's time for both of us to move on and mingle with the other guests. Shall we?"

2. **Signal the close.** "I've enjoyed our conversation. May I follow up with you after the meeting?"

3. **Play the LinkedIn card.** When you are ready to bring the conversation to a close, ask them "Are you on LinkedIn? May I send you an invitation to connect online?"

4. **Take a break.** "If you don't mind, I'm going to get a drink." Or, "If you'll excuse me, the ladies room is calling."

5. **Be a connector.** "Oh, there's Sally Fraser. May I introduce you to her?"

6. **Be humble.** "I have dominated much of your time. You need to meet more people. Thanks for speaking with me."

7. **Add more people to the conversation.** When you sense other people around you, use open body language and hand gestures to invite them into your conversation. When the time is right, leave these two people and move on to another cluster. "I think you two have a lot in common. I'll take my leave so you can get to know each other better."

8. **Excuse yourself.** "If you don't mind, I need to go check on something. I've enjoyed our conversation."

9. **Exchange business cards.** "Before I depart, can we exchange business cards?"

10. **Get the other person's permission.** "I see an old friend that I'd like to reconnect with. Do you mind if I part your company?"

11. **Wish them well.** "I'll take my leave now. I hope you have a great evening and meet many interesting people."

12. **Let them go.** "There are many people here tonight that you'll want to meet. It's been a pleasure connecting with you. Enjoy your evening."

Of course, body language and vocal inflection will be an important part of making any of these responses work. Be careful not to start with scanning eyes—looking around the room to see to whom else you can talk. This sends a very negative message to the person with whom you are currently networking. While you are with that individual, give him or her your full attention. When you decide it's time to move on, do so with respect and dignity.

Now that you know how to more confidently move in and out of conversations at live networking events, let's discuss what you can do if you are having difficulty engaging people and getting them to respond to your calls, e-mails, texts, and social media messages. Are they ignoring you on purpose? The next chapter helps you figure out what to do when you near the black hole of non-response.

> *"There's a trick to the Graceful Exit. I begins with the vision to recognize when a job, a life stage, a relationship is over—and to let go. It means leaving what's over without denying its value."*
> — ELLEN GOODMAN, AMERICAN JOURNALIST, PULITZER PRIZE WINNER FOR DISTINGUISHED COMMENTARY (1980)

21. DETOURS AND DEAD ENDS

*What to Do When the Other Person
is Non-responsive*

You are driving along and everything seems fine. Maybe you don't actually see the sign that says NOT A THROUGH STREET or NO OUTLET or DEAD END. All of the sudden, there's no more road ahead. You can't keep going in the direction that you'd like. You need to either turn around and go back the way you came or you must change course and follow signs that say DETOUR. Who knows how long or how off course this redirection will take you. This experience can certainly be a time waster and a source of frustration.

It happens with people, too. You meet someone networking and you seem to get along pretty well at first. There is a good amount of exchange and interaction and then something changes. Perhaps it becomes obvious: you have a direct conversation about it (usually over e-mail to avoid the conflict; but beware of the easy misinterpretation of the communication). Most of the time people will simply fade away from your network. They stop communicating with you. You wonder if it's just a follow-up issue or are they telling you that they don't want you in their life. Either way, silence sends a powerful signal.

Don't Plow Through

Back to the metaphor: let's say you came upon a blocked road. Maybe there is a downed tree or some obstruction on the road. Would you go around it and continue on your course? What if that fallen tree had taken with it some live electrical lines? Are you willing to risk your life to stay the course?

You may physically be able to go around the blockage, but I recommend against it. The barrier was put up there for a reason. In networking, people have the right to protect themselves and decide who gets in and who doesn't get in to their life. (Read Chapter 9, "The Red Velvet Rope Policy" from Michael Port's *Book Yourself Solid*). Rather than forcing your way in, you need to back off and give the relationship a rest. It needs time. They need time.

Patience and Persistence

Building a relationship is a balancing act. It requires a mix of time, trust, experience, follow-up, and a whole lot of patience on your part. Not every plant is classified as an Annual, purchased from the garden store for instant color or grows quickly from seed and guaranteed to bloom within 40-60 days. Some relationships, like fruit trees, won't be productive for many years. They grow slowly over time, requiring your patience and your care. Some never produce fruit, but look nice and ornamental. They all serve a purpose.

Don't Take it Personally

Remember the concentric circles of "Your Sphere of Influence" in Chapter 3. There's you, your Top 50 contacts, your Active Network, your Lost Network, and your Future Network. People in your network can move between these circles. I just had an experience where someone in my Top 50 contacts elected to move out. It was a mutual decision. Is she gone forever from my life? No. She has just moved out to a different circle, perhaps to the Active Network or maybe even the Lost Network. I am confident that when the time is right, I can reclaim this relationship and reactivate it. Timing is everything.

Networking is an "At Will" Relationship

For some of us more sensitive types, disconnecting from someone in your personal or professional network can make you sad, upset, frustrated, and even angry. It's hard not to take it personally; it's a relationship after all.

I recall one such mystery in my life with a professional associate, let's call her Tina. I had hired Tina and her company to help me develop and launch two corporate websites for two different companies over a period of four years. We had spent a fair amount of time together. I once invited her to an off-sight department retreat where she shared some very helpful advice with me at a very challenging time in my career. Her words of wisdom have stuck with me for years. I considered her a budding mentor at the time.

To my continual surprise, she did not return my phone calls or e-mails… for years. I know that she is still at the same number, because I get her voice mail message, and her administrator still answers her phone. I used to think "Well, she's busy." Then I told myself "Well, she's not very good with follow-up." Or "She's a reluctant networker." But at some point, I came to the conclusion that Tina was choosing not to respond to me. She has chosen an indirect way to communicate with me. She is avoiding me and giving me the "silent treatment." Perhaps the feelings about our relationship weren't mutual. Perhaps she wasn't the mentor that I had hoped she might be. Regardless of what's going on, it's time for me for move on. The relationship with Tina is not worth investing in. I can't explain it. I can't control how Tina responds to me, but I can control what I do with my energy. It's time to let go.

> *In order to keep your professional network healthy and growing, you need to let go of some people in order to acquire better matches for you professionally.*

Can you Say "Next?"

There are several billion people out there in the world—plenty with whom you can build networking relationships. You don't necessarily have to have thick skin, but you do need to embrace the word "next." In order to keep your professional network healthy and growing, you need to let go of some people in order to acquire better matches for you professionally. Call it pruning if you will. You need to develop a disease resistance nature to your professional tree of life. There is strength in moving on. Don't allow yourself to get stuck in unproductive relationships. Learn to dust yourself off, pick yourself up, and start all over again. Look forward and say "next!"

Practice Patience with your Networking Relationships

I recommend that you put some breathing space in your relationships. Be careful not to drown people with too much follow-up. Don't over e-mail or call too frequently. Your enthusiasm, while well intended, may push people away from you. Keep in mind relationships are built over time. Forcing them to move faster than normal (and some make take years to develop) may distort or limit the possibilities. Be patient with your networking relationship and more benefits will come your way.

Learn to Let Go and Move On

Some networking connections are short-lived or have natural limitations. Not all relationships are meant to last forever and be central to your life. It's perfectly okay to have people come and go from your professional life. You can manage this with grace and aplomb, respect and dignity. When one goes, it makes room for another.

Appreciate your present network

Don't over analyze why certain networking relationships didn't work out. Celebrate the ones that do. Make the most of your current and active networking relationships. They will be the key to your future network and your on-going success.

Networking is more like a marathon than a sprint. You have to pace yourself and have enough endurance to cover the many miles ahead. In the next chapter we'll talk about dangers of going too fast in a networking relationship and how that can produce the exact opposite of what you seek.

> "*Yesterday is history. Tomorrow is a mystery. Today is a gift. That's why it's called the present.*"
> — ALICE MORSE EARLE, AMERICAN HISTORIAN AND AUTHOR
> (1851-1911)

22. Odometer versus Speedometer

Gauging the Pace of Your Networking Relationships

Think about the dashboard on your vehicle. How frequently do you look at the speedometer to know how fast you are going at any given moment? It's a point of contention for many drivers who are pulled over by police officers for exceeding the speed limit. We couldn't have been driving that fast!

Driving fast is exciting. You feel as if you are getting somewhere. It makes you feel as if you are the master of your own destiny.

Now think about your odometer. How often do you look at this gauge? How do you feel when you see the miles on your car piling up? Does it make you feel old or worn? You know, closer to that oil change date? Do you feel, with every mile driven, that the resale value of your car is declining?

In networking, these two gauges are also very important: How fast you can build new relationships and how long will those relationships last? Going fast versus going the distance: Which is more important for you in terms of building mutually beneficial relationships?

Find Your Cruise Control

Once you master a few of the networking skills and employ some of the networking strategies that you will discover in this book, you will be able to put your networking efforts on cruise control. That means you'll be able to drive at a reasonable speed—one that is safe and that you consciously choose. You'll get better gas mileage which enables you to drive farther on the same amount of gas. Cruise control will keep you out of traffic court, will reduce the stress on your body while driving, and will help to optimize the performance of your vehicle. What's not to like about cruise control?

What does cruise control look like when you network? It might go something like this:

- You are not rushed to develop the relationship. You take a long-term view of it and build it through time. The value of the connection is not a destination, but rather a journey.

- You are less stressed about the relationship. You discontinue the jerky stop-start motions that you may have done earlier. The relationship building process becomes more fluid and natural for you.

- The process of follow-up is more automatic. You don't really have to think about it; you just let it roll. When you think of this person, you reach out in kindness. You check in more regularly, because you care about the relationship. You are less focused on the immediacy of the networking exchange and more focused on seeing a bigger, longer-term picture.

How fast can you build new relationships and how long will those relationships last? Which is more important to you: going fast or going the distance?

The Dangers of Going Too Fast

Here's a story about how I learned the benefits of using cruise control in my networking strategy. In this particular case, I needed to slow down and not force the relationship in order to ensure its longevity.

I considered my former colleague, Mary Lou, to be a good friend. We had worked together for two years; she was my right hand on the job. I served as a professional reference for her on several occasions.

I admired her many skills and loved to brag about her to potential employers. She also helped me in a very significant way. She hired me as a consultant to help one of her new colleagues prepare for a very important internal presentation. This emergency presentation coaching session became my first success story and laid the foundation for my signature coaching and training program, "The Motivated Presenter."

In my enthusiasm and thirst for business growth, I pushed too hard with Mary Lou. I began to look to our relationship for more business development. Mary Lou was not prepared for that. She reacted very negatively, sending me a stinging email that essentially said "back off." And so I did. I took my foot off the gas pedal and gave it a rest for a while. I allowed time and space to let her irritation with me heal and repair. I checked in with her every few months to see how she was doing. She occasionally responded, and I began to wonder if we were really that close.

Then Mary Lou got laid off, and I was one of the people she called upon for help. She confessed to me that she was a reluctant networker and had realized that this was a big weakness for her. She was gainfully re-employed within six months of losing her last position—not bad given what was going on in the labor market at that time. She told me that the biggest lesson that she had learned in this process was that she must always keep up her networking, when she is working and when she is not. I am optimistic that this lesson will stick with her, and her attitude and behavior about networking have fundamentally and forever changed.

But I also learned a valuable lesson from this experience. You can't expect everyone to give as much as you do or even give what you desperately want and need them to give to you.

The value of the relationship is much bigger than any referral, job assignment, or transaction that may come your way as a result of knowing this person. My behavior and expectations toward Mary Lou put our relationship in jeopardy. I was going too fast and too hard. I needed to back off the gas and adjust to a more comfortable speed for her. As a result, our relationship is still intact. We are having lunch in two weeks.

Going the Distance with Your Relationships

The cool thing about using the cruise control feature when you network is that you can adjust it as you go. You can accelerate and decelerate as you need. If the new networking relationship needs a little more urgency or needs to move at a faster pace, you can easily speed it up. If on the other hand, you sense that your new networking friend is crazy busy and time-starved, you might want to back off a bit, slow it down and let the relationship take more time to develop. Your goal is to become a long-distance driver and networker. You are going the distance with all the relationships you build. You want a high reading on your networking odometer!

> *"Don't brag about your lightning pace, for Slow and Steady won the race!"*
>
> — AESOP, ANCIENT GREEK FABULIST AND STORY TELLER

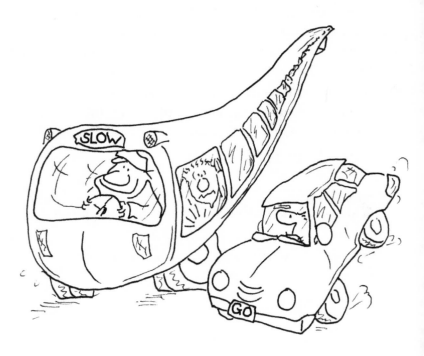

Checklist #3

You are almost there! You've completed Part III of your networking journey. Part IV will give you resources and inspiration to make you a motivated networker for life. Complete this checklist and you will be ready for Part IV.

☐ I know what to do to turn a new connect into a meaningful connection. I actively work to progress relationships through the Networking Funnel of Opportunity.

☐ I understand how to leverage networking as part of my business development strategy. I am confident in discussing business opportunities with people in my professional network.

☐ I regularly ask other people that I know to help me by facilitating warm introductions to new people that I wish to add to my network.

☐ I have a strong presence on the major social media sites. I have completed my profile and uploaded a professional-looking photograph so people can easily recognize me. I actively invite people to connect and interact with me using online channels.

☐ I have mastered the art of conversation and know that listening and asking questions are important in the communication and relationship-building process. I keep my ego and "I-messages" in check and focus more of my energy on getting to know other people.

PART IV

Arriving at Your Destination
Take Your Networking to the Next Level

23. Park Next to the Lamborghini

*Networking with People with Money,
Power, and Influence*

Do you consider yourself rich? Could you stand to be richer? Of course you could. But we can and should define wealth in broader terms, not just financially. There's the wealth of good health and vitality. You cannot buy it. There's the wealth of strong, loving, and healthy relationships. There are riches that come from possessing a good attitude and having imagination and creativity at your disposal. There's the power of positive motivation and determination—that's worth a fortune. And then, yes, there's money, assets, and access to them.

No matter what your current circumstance in life, no matter how many miles your odometer shows, you too have the opportunity to stretch out of your comfort zone and start networking with people of greater influence and resource than you presently have. The reality is you must, if you want to go anywhere and do anything significant with your life and career.

When I lived and worked in Europe during the mid-1990's, I was always surprised when I would run up against classism—the societal struggle between the "haves" and "have-nots." It's a classic cultural divide that has lasted for eons in virtually every nation on earth. Yet some people manage to overcome it and leapfrog from their current station in life to new, higher levels.

In this age of information and technology, where innovation and motivation can triumph against any obstacle, real or imagined, we all have the potential for greatness. But it takes a great deal of gumption to go and get it. And you can achieve that through your professional networking.

Consider a young teenager named Jackson (not his real name). At the time of this writing, he was a senior at a magnet school in Connecticut. I met Jackson while I was teaching a networking class to the school's film class, as part of my community service. I was actually doing a favor for a networking friend and fellow Soroptimist, Sharon, and her incredible husband. They are involved with the school as members of the Business Community Advisory Board, which creates internships, mentoring, and other resources for the economically underprivileged, but highly motivated and brilliant students at the school.

Jackson was one of the first students to greet me. He was personable, confident, and handsome. I recall that he gave me a firm, professional handshake and made direct eye contact while he introduced himself. These are qualities and actions I always admire—regardless of age. Jackson quickly expressed his personal brand when he threw me an odd-ball question during Q&A. He asked me if I knew a good recipe for guacamole. This was precisely the kind of question that the teacher had warned the kids not to ask their guest speaker. But I fell for it and started listing off ingredients to make the perfect dip. I saw Jackson again at the annual Business Partnership Breakfast, where he was serving as the master of ceremonies. Once again, he was charismatic, confident, bold, and prepared. When the school principal spoke, he mentioned that Jackson would always have a place in his heart because he was the first student to welcome him to the new school and to shake his hand. Jackson had figured out at the age of fifteen that parking next to the Lamborghini is smart. Why not the rest of us adults?

> *It takes a great deal of gumption to go and get it. And you can achieve that through your professional networking.*

Step Up Your Game

If you are serious about creating strong career and business success for yourself, you must step out of your comfort zone and start networking with people of greater influence than you. You will need people with more resources (including higher-level connections and relationships) to get you introduced and exposed to higher-level opportunities. Waiting in line with everyone else may be the polite thing to do, but you'll be waiting for a long time and you may not get your turn. You need greater access. You need to associate with people who can connect you to the right places and leaders. It's time to accelerate and supercharge your networking efforts.

Here are a few things you can do to get yourself into position for people of influence to advocate for you:

1. **Do your research.** Know who's who in your targeted community. Find out the details including their background, their families, their hobbies, and interests, the things that they like and don't like. Who is currently connected to them? Where do they hang out?

2. **Be where they congregate.** Invest in purchasing tickets to the charity events, conferences, golf and social clubs they are known to frequent. Make an investment in your own career by purchasing access to the places where they gather. Perhaps you have to start out as a golf caddy, but at least you'll have close personal time with them and know their strengths and weaknesses.

3. **Ask for what you need.** Practice making your pitch before the real thing. Make it crisp and compelling. Make it short. Give the person a powerful reason to help you. Be persistent. Don't take no for an answer. You may irritate the individual, but he or she will admire your tenacity. This is the trait of a leader.

> *"If you want to go somewhere, it is best to find someone who has already been there."*
> —ROBERT KIYOSAKI, AUTHOR OF *RICH DAD POOR DAD*

Join the Board

People of money and influence often have a philanthropic spirit. They feel compelled to give back. They also enjoy the political and social power and visibility that comes with being on nonprofit boards of directors and committees. That's a great place to meet them. They are more open to new ideas and new people. They are out of their traditional work environment and are less likely to block your entrance.

By signing on as a board member or committee member, you may also benefit from the richness of mission-driven work. What might have started as a professional networking motivation or desire for status in the community will soon morph into something bigger and even more meaningful. You will be on a path of giving back and serving the greater good. This is when you will be at your very best and will become naturally attractive to people of power and influence.

You must let your intentions be known and ask to be considered to nonprofit board positions. And you must be willing to carve out significant time and energy to devote to and fulfill this new community leadership role. Your performance in this capacity will be a demonstration of your worth to the people with whom you are trying to connect. Once you earn their trust, they will open their "Rolodex" of people of influence and resource to you.

Finally, you must be patient—very patient. People of money, power, and influence are used to people sucking up to them and seeking them out. They are in demand, not because they are wonderful people, but because they can provide for others. It is natural that they are cautious and suspicious. Your approach to them must be authentic, professional, and positive. They will quickly sniff out the fakes, phonies, and fearful.

Respectfully Equal

It is important that you present yourself as a confident person who is capable of providing good value. You too have resources and the ability and willingness to help others, just as they do. Your body language and use of voice must convey strength. Eye contact is critically important, as is your handshake. For these two nonverbal actions will send an instant signal to the powerful person with whom you want to connect. Your bank balance may currently be less than theirs, but your self-esteem and belief in your intrinsic self-worth is on par or better. You are not afraid to hear "no" because you know that "no" is a power word, and you respect it highly. If someone is unwilling or unable to help you, muster the courage to ask if they know anyone else who might be in a position to assist you. Try this line: "Is there someone else in your network who you think would be a good connection for me?" If they say yes, then ask, "Great. Would you be willing to facilitate an introduction for me? How can I make that easy for you to do?"

Ultimately, you both put your pants on the same way—one leg at a time. You both have the same organs—heart, lungs, kidney, liver, etc. You are both equally susceptible to disease, illness, and heartache. You both have the opportunity for greatness in what you personally achieve and whom else you help to achieve it. You both have something to gain by helping each other in networking.

> *If you are serious about creating strong career and business success for yourself, you must step out of your comfort zone and start networking with people of greater influence.*

Now that you are feeling fearless, unintimidated by people with money and power, it's time to open it up a little more. This next chapter embraces the ABCs of networking—Always Be Connecting. You will discover that any place or space that people gather is an opportunity for networking. Let's see what this thing can do off road.

> *"Position yourself as a center of influence—the one who knows the movers and shakers. People will respond to that, and you'll soon become what you project."*
> — BOB BURG, AUTHOR OF *THE GO-GIVER*

24. Off-Roading

Unusual Places to Network

If you are open to it, any event and any location can become a networking opportunity. Now, this does not mean that you have to constantly be hustling or have your business hat on. After all, this could become annoying to the other people in your life, like your spouse. "Do you always have to bring up business?" With the right approach, anywhere there are people, there is an opportunity to have a conversation that could lead to a future relationship that just might benefit your career and business or that of someone you know. That's the magic of networking.

Lesson from a Movie

I am thinking of the 2004 movie *Open Water*, a terrifying film based upon true events of a married couple that gets left behind on a scuba diving trip while vacationing in the Caribbean. The film is loosely based on the true story of Tom and Eileen Lonergan, who in 1998, went out with a scuba diving group on the Great Barrier Reef in Australia, and were accidentally left behind because the dive-boat crew failed to take an accurate headcount. The movie shows them alone at sea, soon to die horrible deaths. I often think if this couple had done a little networking while on the boat ride out, instead of just keeping to themselves, people would have noticed that they were not on board when the boat departed back for shore. Who knows, networking could literally save your life.

{ *Anywhere there are people, there is an opportunity to have a conversation that could lead to a future relationship. That's the magic of networking.* }

Networking While on Vacation

One very memorable vacation that my husband Byron and I took was a trip to Peru to hike the Inca Trail leading to Machu Picchu. It was Byron's 40th birthday and we wanted to do something big. At first, the idea of backpacking in a foreign country and sleeping outdoors without access to proper showers and toilets was a bit off-putting to me. I have come to accept the fact that I am more of a Marriott hotel kind of traveler. Not so for my adventurous husband. But it was his birthday and the least I could do was to accompany him and leave my complaints behind. In fact, that was my actual birthday promise to him "I'll go on this trip and not complain, not once." I am pleased to report that I honored that promise and had a fantastic trip to this incredible part of the world. It was one of the highlights of my life.

I hadn't anticipated that I would come away from this adventure with new professional and personal connections that would last for many years. It's hard not to get close to people, when you are schlepping up and down mountains for four days, eating meals together, and spending evenings in conversation because there wasn't much else to do. On this trip, I met Bronwyn and Charlie, an inspiring couple with very interesting careers. Bronwyn, who we called Marie because no one could remember how to say her name properly, was celebrating her 50th birthday on this trip. She was an inspiration to me: physically strong, real, professionally accomplished, smart, kind, and fun. She was a research and development scientist working in the food industry. This fascinated me. Over the course of four days through our various adventures and vistas, I got to spend some time with her and her husband, Charlie. Fifteen years later, we are still in touch with them…only now I know how to spell and pronounce her real name. Our connection is a hybrid between personal and professional. I'm curious as to when and how our connection will lead to professional opportunities for ourselves or others that we know. Time (and follow-up) will tell.

Networking at Special Events

Celebrations are a natural place for people to connect. That includes baptisms, birthday parties, graduations, weddings, Bar Mitzvah/Bat Mitzvah, and yes, even funerals (or celebrations of life, as I like to call them). Let me share a story of how I gained two wonderful new connections at a funeral.

My dear friend, former client, and mentor, Richard "Dick" Adams passed away after a brief battle with cancer in June 2015. He has just moved from Connecticut to Minnesota to be closer to his children and grandchildren. He called me about one month after arriving there with the news of his cancer diagnosis. I vowed to myself that I'd try to help him and his family in any way that I could. When his wife Pat called me to tell me that Dick had passed, I was heartbroken. I made it a point to attend his funeral services which were held in Connecticut where Dick had some many friends and associates. There I met his daughter Beth and son David, and his many vivacious grandchildren. I shared a special story with Beth and David about the first time I met their father and the kindness he bestowed on me when I was just starting out in my new business. We agreed to stay in touch. Several months later I had the opportunity to go to Minneapolis on a business trip. I made it a point to contact Pat and suggest a lunch with her adult children, Beth and David. We had a marvelous time over lunch and conversation. Learning that David was accomplished business development strategist with a special interest in productivity and effectiveness, I invited him to be a guest contributor to my blog. In September 2015, he wrote a compelling piece about how we over-use the word "busy" and confuse it as a sign of success. You can read his article entitled "Going Out of Busy-ness" by David Lindsay Adams at: americasmarketingmotivator. com/going-out-of-busy-ness

Just like his father, David has inspired me to think differently about how I view my time, my progress, and the value of my life. And to think that I met him at a funeral of all places. Networking magic can happen anywhere.

Networking at College Reunions

Most people I know hate the thought of college reunions. It makes them incredibly self-conscious of their bodies, their age, their hair or absence of it! They are worried about how people will judge their accomplishments or lack thereof. Many people want to put those college memories behind them. They are now a different person altogether and what was important back then is no longer relevant. Times have changed.

This is exactly why you should go to your next college reunion. Times have changed and this creates the perfect opportunity for you to re-calibrate your relationships. You also have the opportunity to meet new people and establish new connections that could prove to be helpful to you in the future.

A few years back, I attended my 25th college reunion at Stanford University. I had missed my 20th reunion and received "guilt mail" from my dorm mates wondering where the heck I was. In truth, I was hiding in my pity party having recently lost my job and not feeling particularly confident. In hindsight, I should have gone. It could have jumpstarted my new beginning.

Nevertheless, I made the investment of time, money and energy and I showed up to my 25th reunion. It was fantastic. The campus had changed so much with new buildings dedicated to every technology superstar from the Silicon Valley and beyond. There was the Bill Gates computer building. David Packard and Bill Hewitt of HP each had their own building. Jerry Yang, co-founder of Yahoo had his own facility as well. I strolled down memory lane and walked amongst new places and spaces. It was energizing. But the most meaningful moments for me were the quiet coffees and lunches with old friends. Catching up on their lives and learning about their future ambitions was so enriching. I feel closer to my old friends Jeff and Gordon and Doug and Fran. I got to know Buffy from a new perspective and now we are in touch via Facebook. Fiona is rocking and rolling and Maggie and her amazing husband Mark are an inspiring team. I had the opportunity to attend a special workshop, facilitated by my former classmate Andy Chan, on finding your purpose in life and work. Andy has a brilliant mind and is a compassionate person. It was awesome to observe him in this leadership role. He works at Wakeforest University in North Carolina, where he leads innovation and career development for students and alumni. Andy is clearly someone to stay in touch with.

I even met a gentleman on the campus bus on the way to the alumni parking lot. He was older than I was and from a different culture and a different graduating class, but we had something in common: we both had Stanford in our blood. We had a conversation about our current work focus and our involvement in non-profit organizations. He runs a major strategic consulting firm serving global non-profits organizations like UNICEF. I found that fascinating. We exchanged business cards and we followed up in the weeks following the reunion. A new networking connection had been established. It may or may not result in any business opportunities. It was definitely worth the effort of extending myself to a stranger, who now is part of my professional network. Of course, this wouldn't have been possible if I hadn't shown up at my college reunion.

Why You Might Want to Attend a Convention or Conference

Another good opportunity to practice your networking skills and acquire new connections is by attending a large conference or convention. You can attend as a guest, as an exhibitor, as a sponsor, or as a speaker. There are many roles that you can play and each one comes with the opportunity to network with new people.

The key to networking success at conventions and conferences is preparation and follow up. Here's what I do:

- **Do pre-work a few weeks before the conference.** Find out who's going to the conference. Ask the organizers for a copy of the registration list (or if it's posted online or on social media). Let people know you plan on attending the conference by sharing on social media (include a link to the conference website). Reach out directly to a few of the registered attendees in advance to start the rapport building process. I do this one of three ways: 1) send them a LinkedIn invitation or message (if we are already connected online) telling them that I will also be at the conference and would love to meet up with them; 2) call them on the phone to introduce myself, let them know that I'll be at the conference and see if we could set a time to get together. Of course, you must prepare yourself to leave an effective voice mail message; and 3) If I can find their mailing address, I might send them a handwritten note (or creative travel postcard from the city where the conference will be held) telling them that I'll be there and would love to meet with them.

- **Bring plenty of business cards with you to the conference.** In fact, bring more than you think you'll need. If your company doesn't provide one, then have one printed at local office supply retail, like Staples or online at VistaPrint.com. Your business card should contain all of your contact details in type that is big enough for people to read. Leave some white space on the card somewhere so that they can take notes. There is no excuse for forgetting your business cards. Just like your credit card—don't leave home without it.

- **During the conference, make an effort to meet a handful (or more) of people.** Get to know them through short but meaningful conversation, suggest that you exchange business cards, and confidently ask for their permission to connect with them after the event. Be sure to jot down a few notes on the back of the business card while the memory is still fresh. I like to write down the date, conference name, and a keyword or two to remind me of our conversation. This memory-jogging information is very helpful when you begin to complete your personalized follow-up.

- **Follow-up quickly after the event.** Time block a few hours on your calendar following the conference to ensure you complete the follow-up actions and any promises you made. This is where most people fall down. They come home with tons of business cards and then just add them to the pile of clutter on the desk. I recommend that you follow up within 24-48 hours after the conference. You can send a LinkedIn invitation, e-mail them, text them, send them a handwritten note (with another copy of your business card tucked in), or call them in a few days to suggest ways you might be able to help each other.

- **Do a second follow-up about six to eight weeks later.** You can reach out with a LinkedIn message, e-mail, or phone call. Remind them where you met (just in case they have forgotten you). Ask them what's new in their life. Let them know that you are happy to help them or anyone else in their network.

Leave your phone and e-mail contact details so they can easily contact you.

Conventions and conferences can be exhausting, physically as well as mentally and emotionally. This is especially true for people with introverted personalities. It is essential that you take care of yourself. Let's start with the basics. Wearing sensible shoes is an obvious piece of advice that many people overlook. You will be on your feet much of the day. You also want to be sure not to carry too much stuff with you, like heavy briefcases, large purses, or computers. Go light and mobile, as this will free up your hands to shake with others and puts less strain on your back and shoulders.

Make sure that you eat well during the conference. You'll need energy, and a steady diet of coffee or colas is not the answer. In fact, water would be a better choice of beverage during such events. A healthy breakfast is essential. Avoid the garbage snack foods that they sell at most conventions. This will only drain your energy.

If you need a rest break, take one. Don't keep going until you drop. Step outside the building every few hours to get some fresh air. Do some stretching to loosen your muscles. This is very important to ensure that you are in the best state of mind and body when you present yourself and your ideas to others at the conference or convention.

If you start to feel overwhelmed, shy, or reluctant (and you'll know this is happening because you'll start to withdraw into your smartphone), take a moment to pump yourself up again. This is a challenging environment, and probably everyone in the building is feeling the same as you. Give yourself a pep talk and remind yourself that you are here to meet new people and network and that someone you meet today might very well become your future client, your future business partner, a future investor, or a future friend. It is worth the effort of your time and energy. Put yourself out there and in position for good things to happen to you and your career.

Network Anytime, Anywhere

Wherever people gather, there is an opportunity to connect. It does not have to be an official sanctioned networking event. With a small dose of curiosity, some conversation skills, and the willingness to take a risk, you just might find yourself making new connections. And who knows where that might lead you.

It just might turn you into a master connector, an individual who has an uncanny ability to put people together in a way that creates new opportunities for many. Would you like to be that kind of driver?

> *"Straight roads do not make skillful drivers."*
> — PAULO COELHO, BRAZILIAN LYRICIST AND NOVELIST, INCLUDING ONE OF THE BEST-SELLING BOOKS IN HISTORY, *THE ALCHEMIST*

25. Drivers Wanted

Be a Connector of People

You often hear companies proclaiming, "People are our most important assets." Yet many of their organizational policies and practices are often in direct conflict with this core value. The same holds true for people and networking. We say people are important to us, but then we take them for granted, ignore them for long periods of time, and reach out to them only when we need them. This is not walking the talk.

The graduate level of networking is when you become a master connector—a person of influence who connects other people together. You actively share your connections with others, and encourage them to meet and get to know each other. You are the talent development director and a relationship management specialist. You see the potential magic that is possible when the right people come together. And you are the kind of person who makes that happen frequently.

When you do this, you will not only have developed a new core competency (i.e., people skills), but also you will have a valuable new asset on your balance sheet—more fans.

This section is focused on how you can become a connector by adopting simple practices and a shift in mindset.

Seeing the Connections

When you network with people, you need to use your peripheral vision. You need to be actively thinking about who this person should be meeting with after you. Who else do you know who would benefit from meeting this person, or who else do you know whom this person could help? You need to be scanning for similarities, including shared values, interests, and experiences. This is the basis of a good networking connection—people with common ground.

For example, I met Jennifer Keohane when she was the business outreach librarian at the Simsbury Public Library in Connecticut. Jennifer connected me to many people. She was instrumental in helping me launch my new business back in 2005. Jennifer is definitely a master connector, and the people in her network benefit greatly from her networking skill, business savvy, and open heart. Of all the connections Jennifer made for me none was as important as Pamela (Pam) Lacko. It turns out that Pam and I have a few things in common: we both live in the same town, we are both business owners, and we both are ovarian cancer survivors. Jennifer's timely and kindly introduction of Pam to me was paramount in my cancer survivorship. Pam gave me ideas on how to get through chemotherapy sessions with a sense of humor intact. You see, Pam is the author of *Laughing in the Face of Cancer*. Her courage, creativity, and comradery continue to inspire me to live well. This blessing came to my life because Jennifer Keohane is a master connector.

When you become a master connector, you will find that you start to do this naturally. You just think this way. It's an unconscious competence that you possess. Other people you network with are not yet at this level. Your initiative to help introduce them to others is, in essence, modeling excellence. You understand at a deep level that putting people and ideas together is a powerful thing to do. You see beyond yourself. You are future-oriented. You are willing to help other people, even if they are reluctant or afraid to meet other people.

> *The graduate level of networking is when you become a master connector—a person of influence who connects other people together.*

Facilitating New Introductions

One way you can help people in your network is to facilitate introductions for them. What do I mean by that? You help people relax and get to know each other when they are meeting for the first time. You take the burden of starting the conversation between them. You get things going.

Here are a few ways in which you can easily do this:

- **Live and In Person.** You can do this at a party or meeting, when you are face-to-face, by intentionally setting out to introduce your friend to other people. You help to position that person well by stating a few things that the individual might have a hard time saying about himself or herself. Act as a publicity agent and give testimony about what you value about your friend.

- **Three-Way.** If you host a three-way lunch, three-way coffee or three-way dinner, you are bringing two people together with you to help oversee it. This requires a little more investment of your time and energy (and sometimes your money), but you will benefit as well. This approach ensures that the connection actually happens. It goes better when you bring these two people together and help to facilitate their conversation. You strengthen your relationship with both of them, and get the joy of seeing a little networking magic happen. Try it out.

- **Phone.** You can facilitate introductions over the phone. You can call both parties and let them know you'd like to introduce them to each other. Get their verbal agreement, and alert them that you'll be sending their contact details via e-mail. Or if you have three-way conference calling, you could do it live on the spot. This can work magic, but, conversely, it can put people on the spot when they are not ready to talk.

- **E-mail.** You can facilitate introductions through e-mail by writing to both parties and encouraging them to connect. I like to provide basic contact details such as e-mail and telephone numbers to make connecting convenient. I also write a few sentences about why I think they would make a good connection. I wish them "happy networking" and invite them to let me know how it goes. Please note: The probability of people acting on an e-mail introduction is lower than if you do it in person or over the telephone. It's easier to ignore e-mails, you might be catching the person at a very busy time, or be the 110th e-mail in their inbox. It's easy for e-mail to get lost.

- **Social Media.** You can also introduce people via LinkedIn and other social media sites. LinkedIn has a function called "Share profile," where you can forward the profile link of someone you know and trust to someone else in your LinkedIn network who would be a good match. You can also request new connections using the "Get Introduced through a Connection" functionality. Both of these approaches require that you write a personal introduction. I have had success using both but do find that it is still fairly passive, and most people are slow to respond.

Networking Introductions via E-mail

Here's an example of an e-mail introduction I facilitated. I have left blank lines for their last names, contact information, and other sensitive information, out of respect for their privacy.

> Networking introduction: Pat meet Louise. Louise meet Pat
>
> I love connecting powerful women, especially when they both work for the same organization...and in the same location.
>
> Pat – Please meet Louise _____. She and I have both served

on the board of the _____, and are members of its Development Committee. Louise is a marketing guru, and currently deploys LEAN Continuous Improvement efforts throughout your company.

Louise's e-mail _____

Louise's work tele _____

Louise's LinkedIn profile URL _____

Louise please meet Patricia (Pat) _____. Pat and I met at the Business Women's Forum some years back and have developed a special connection (her daughter and I share the same birthday). Pat is an actuary with a head for making sense of data. She is also a huge supporter of women and serves as a volunteer leader for the _____ Women's Network. She hired me to speak at the group's annual meeting. Pat and I also recently had dinner together near your _____ office.

Pat's work tele _____

Pat's e-mail _____

Pat's LinkedIn profile _____

Please take time to connect with each other and get to know each other. Perhaps over lunch?

Happy Networking. Let me know how it goes.

Kathy McAfee
America's Marketing Motivator
Talk/Text to my mobile: (860) 371-8801
E-mail me at Kathy@AmericasMarketingMotivator.com

Louise responded almost immediately to my e-mail with this message:

> "Ha! Kathy, you are too much. Thank you for the invite. I'll connect here with Pat, and we'll have coffee or lunch."

Curious how things developed, I reached out to see what if anything actually happened. I spoke on the phone separately with Louise and Pat exactly 499 days after I first connected them over e-mail. I was delighted to learn that they acted on my introduction, and have met several times. As a result of putting these two talented career professionals together, some wonderful things happened:

1. Their professional networks grew

2. They facilitated introductions to other important people

3. They supported and encouraged each other with career stories and advice

4. They exchanged ideas and explored different ways to partner together

5. Pat was promoted and now is in position to mentor, sponsor, and advocate for more people

6. They each made a new friend

Louise and Pat both expressed interest in staying connected. I gave them a few ideas on how they could do that in a creative and personal way. I have full confidence that they will continue to invest in this professional relationship, resulting in even more reward and joy.

It takes effort to build a relationship,
but it is always worth it.

You are welcome to replicate my formula or create your own. But your job as a master connector is to make it easy and inviting to act on your introductions. I even have a folder in my e-mail account called Networking where I store these introductory e-mails. That way I can check back and see who has acted on them, and who needs another nudge.

Be the Host

One of the easiest ways to get comfortable in networking and to improve your connecting skills is to practice the strategy called "Be the Host." It works like this: Whenever you go to a meeting, conference, or gathering of people, pretend that it is your party and you are the host. As the host, it is your job to make sure your guests are welcomed, introduced around, and are having a good time. It would be rude of you to spend all of your time with just one guest, so it is expected that you will mingle among all your guests. If it were your party, you would take a more active role in introducing people to each other. You'd be facilitating introductions.

When you act the host, you have a higher energy level and a more welcoming demeanor. You are less nervous or worried about yourself. You are unlikely to be the "wall flower," shy and reserved. And you also are doing great service to the official host by helping to start conversations and ensuring the guests are enjoying themselves. The gathering is more likely to be successful because of your efforts. You might just find that you are invited to more events!

Get a Seat at the Table

When you become a connector of people and expand your sphere of influence, you will have an easier time getting a seat at the table. You'll be invited to participate in higher-level meetings, organizing committees, and other places and spaces where people of influence gather. By showcasing your people skills and natural ability to bring people together, others will see you as a leader. You will have secured yourself a seat at the table for more interesting conversations.

The best personal example of this is my work and involvement with the YWCA Hartford Region in Connecticut. The YWCA is the oldest and largest multicultural, multigenerational women's organization in the world. I met the wonderful people of the YWCA through a networking connection facilitated through my career coach at an outplacement agency. Rhonda LoBrutto introduced me to her friend Debra (Palermino) Palmer, who, at the time, was serving as the chairwoman of the board of directors of the YWCA, in addition to running her own consultancy firm. Debra graciously invited Rhonda and me to be her table guests at the YWCA's In the Company of Women luncheon, a fabulous fund raising luncheon that is packed with 1,500 women and men from the community who are motivated to help fulfill the YWCA's mission of empowering women and eliminating racism. It was a grand day, and, of course, I followed up to thank Debra and Rhonda for the opportunity.

Debra then facilitated an introduction with Deborah Ullman, the interim executive director of the YWCA. Later Deborah was promoted to CEO and faithfully served for ten years before retiring. At Debra's suggestion, I agreed to do a little pro-bono work for the organization. It then turned into a short marketing engagement—my second client after I had launched my new business. This was a wonderful way to get to know what the organization stood for and to understand the tremendous value that their programs and services provide to our community. I also met fabulous people on their board of directors, their staff, and their donors and supporters. Between their mission and their leaders, it was hard not to get the YWCA fever. I became a passionate advocate.

Within a year, I was nominated for a seat on their board of directors. I served on the board for six years. I met very influential and interesting people—all who share my passion for helping to improve the lives of women and girls (who, in turn, help improve the lives of families, communities, and the world). This step up in exposure, learning, and connections has been phenomenal. And it all started with a facilitated introduction by my career coach Rhonda to Debra, a woman who was a stranger to me at the time. These two women gave me a seat at the table. It can happen to you too.

Meeting Important People

You meet important people when you become an important person. And you never quite know when that is going to happen. But I can tell you how it will happen.

- **You become an important person when you help other people achieve their goals.** You become important to them when your relationship goes from casual acquaintance to strategic friend. You have gained mutual trust through time and they are now comfortable opening their "Rolodex" to you. They advocate for you. They introduce you to people whom you otherwise might not know or might have a hard time meeting by yourself.

- **You become an important person when you realize that you too are important.** This starts with the basic assumption that you are valuable, regardless of your current circumstances. It's called self-esteem. You have to have it. It is the bone marrow of your self-confidence. If you don't have self-esteem or an intrinsic belief in your self-worth, then your body language will show weakness. Your voice will have a quality about it that suggests it's not worth spending time with you. Your inner critic may take over and influence your choice of words when you make that all important call. You have to be confident in how you approach other important people. *So here it is: You are an important person. I bequeath you. I knight you. I give you the crown. Wear it well.*

- **You become an important person when you make more of others' time.** Important people are in demand. Because of their position, authority, influence, power, resources, and connections, many people want a piece of their time and attention (and sometimes their money). Everyone wants time from important people, and that's something that they have little to spare. Therefore, you shouldn't waste their time; rather, you should be strategically thoughtful about how you could help them so that they get more of what they want. At the end of the day, important people are people, too. They have needs. They have feelings. They have challenges. They have dreams and goals, too. You can become important by fulfilling these needs.

- **You become an important person when you have new ideas and take calculated risks to challenge a dysfunctional status quo.** Important people are inundated with yes people. You know the people who agree with you all day long just to stay on your good side. Leaders eventually get bored with the yes people and seek out people who will challenge their thinking. The people closest to them have the most to risk and have the hardest time doing this. But you, as a new connection, have nothing to lose and everything to gain. Be bold. Be helpful and stretch this leader's thinking. You may find yourself becoming valuable to an important person whom you want to add to your professional network.

{ *You meet important people when you become an important person.* }

Teaching Others

When you become a connector of people, you will take on the role of teacher and mentor. You will be guiding others in the art of networking and helping to acquire this valuable professional skill. Your example will help them to adopt a more positive attitude toward meeting people and building relationships through networking. You will be giving back to others in ways that will surprise you. All the while, you and your business will continue to grow as a result of your skilled networking. You are leading and prospering by example.

But even master connectors need to have a game plan. They must plot a course with specific tasks and actions to keep them moving forward. The next chapter will give you some practical and tactical suggestions to help you map out your networking next steps.

> *"Networking is not just about connecting people. It's about connecting people with people, people with ideas, and people with opportunities."*
> —MICHELE JENNAE, AUTHOR OF *THE CONNECTWORKER*

26. Plot Your Course

Design Your Own Networking Roadmap

There are many different ways of traveling. Some people, like my husband, Byron, have a spontaneous "Go North" attitude. Others, like me, like to map out every detail, be highly organized, and know exactly what comes next. Perhaps this is the "perceiver" and the "judger" aspect of the Myers-Briggs Type Indicator (MBTI) where your personality comes shining through. Whatever your style, you can benefit from developing an action plan around your networking goals. Why? Because for most people, networking is not part of their normal routine, and, as such, it becomes a low priority, if not a completely ignored strategy. This entire book has been about heightening your awareness and increasing your motivation toward making networking a key strategy now and for the rest of your life.

What Are Your Networking Goals?

What do you want to achieve with your networking relationships? Why and how can they serve you? What other goals are they connected to? By setting goals, and making them SMART goals (more on that later), you are more likely to achieve success. Once you taste a little success in networking, your confidence builds, and you begin to do it more often. Success begets success. You build momentum in your networking. Before you know it, you can become a master connector.

Building SMART Networking Goals

The SMART goal system means that you set goals that are: Specific, Measurable, Attainable, Realistic, and Timely. This is different from setting BHAG goals: Big, Hairy, Audacious goals. Both types of goals are important and have their place. However, in order to start the momentum-building process in your networking, I recommend that you start a bit more grounded in your approach and leave the lofty, stratospheric goals for another time.

Can you determine which of the following networking goal statements qualify as a SMART goal?

1. Network with top executives who can help me grow my business.

2. Connect with all of the Fortune 500 company leaders who are located in my state.

3. Meet and network with five of the top 20 Fortune 500 company executives who reside in my state by December 31st or sooner.

Now all three of these goal statements are positive and on target; however, the third one is the most "doable." This is because it was written with the SMART goals in mind. Notice the dates and numbers and reasonableness of the goal. It is still a stretch goal, but is much more attainable than the idea of meeting all of the leaders. You can see the natural next step of research to identify the list of the Fortune 500 companies with offices in the state and the executives in charge. Getting to this level of specificity will greatly increase the probability of you achieving this important goal.

Once you taste a little success in networking, your confidence builds, and you begin to do it more often. Success begets success.

Now that You Have Your Goals, What Do You Do Next?

Congratulations! You have written down your networking goals and have put them through the SMART goal test. You have refined them so that they are specific, measurable, achievable, realistic, and timely. Your next step is to build a strategy to achieve it. Strategy is all about the how. Networking and relationship-building are in themselves a strategy, but we don't want to stop there. We want to drill down and get very specific on the how. This is where the action plan comes into play:

- **Goal:** Meet and network with five of the top 20 Fortune 500 company executives who reside in my state by December 31st or sooner.

- **Strategy:** Leverage my professional network to get introduced to these executives.

- **Action plan:**

  1. **Research:** Conduct research to learn more about these companies and executives. Short-list the names to the top 10 who appear to be the best fit for me and what I have to offer. Timing: Complete research by [specific date].

  2. **Who knows whom?** Use LinkedIn to find out who in my network is connected to anyone at these companies or who personally knows these executives. Timing: Complete this step by [specific date].

  3. **Share:** Talk about my specific goal with my Top 50 most important networking contacts. Let them know what I am doing and why, and ask them if they know anyone who could help me achieve this. Follow up on any and all leads or connections they provide to me. Timing: Ongoing activity.

4. **Connect with influencers:** Make connections and network with people who know these executives well and could introduce me in the future. Get to know these influencers, and build trust with them, for they too will add value to my network. Demonstrate my value to these influencers by offering to help them achieve their networking goals. Timing: as opportunities present themselves.

5. **Be patient:** Be persistent. Be flexible. Visualize goal achievement. Timing: This will be an ongoing, daily activity.

6. **Build rapport:** When I meet these executives, I will focus first on rapidly building rapport with them. I will let them know succinctly who I am and what my specialty is. I will listen intently for their needs, pain points, and hot buttons. Find out their birthdays (research online or just ask), and take note of what is important to them personally and professionally. I will plant seeds and ask for their permission to stay in touch over time. Timing: Immediate, in the moment.

7. **Follow up:** After I have met these executives, I will have a game plan for how I can stay visible and valuable to them. I will showcase my uniqueness and motivation by sending personalized cards every three months or so. And I will be relevant and ready for when their timing is right. Timing: First follow up within three days of meeting; thereafter, touch base quarterly.

What if You Are Just Getting Started?

Perhaps you are not planning on taking over the world and want a less intense action plan. No worries. We can handle that. In fact, there are a number of basic action steps you can take to prepare yourself to become more connected and more influential in time.

Here is a suggested three-month action plan that anybody can do to get the networking process rolling. All it takes is a little discipline, time, and persistent motivation.

Three Month Action Plan

1st Month: Desired outcomes: Identify your active network, and create your online presence.

Week #1: Make a list of everyone you know. Use the "My World Exercise" spreadsheet to group people by affiliation and connection to your life. (Download a free template at AmericasMarketingMotivator.com.) In this step, you just need their names. Don't waste your time searching for their contact information. That will come later.

Week #2: Give thought to which of these connections is most important to you. With whom do you have the closest relationships? Who can help you the most? Who are the most connected and influential people you know? Whom do you care about the most? Are those feelings mutual? Would they return your phone calls promptly? From your master list, select the people who fit this description. This is the beginning of your Top 50 contact list.

Week #3: Set yourself up on LinkedIn, Twitter, and Facebook. Include a professional photograph. If you don't have one, get one (no selfies). Fill in your profile with sufficient background information including the jobs you've held, the schools you've attended, and your affiliations. If you need examples of how to craft your profile, check out other people's public profiles. Your profile is an expression of your personal brand; give it some reflection. Remember, you can always modify it in the future. This is the beauty of online platforms.

Week #4: Research different contact management systems. Select one that is right for you. Begin to input the contact details into your system from your "My World Exercise" spreadsheet. Invite these same people to link in with you on LinkedIn. If you don't have their full updated contact information, ask for it, so that you can input it into your contact management system.

2nd Month: Desired outcomes: Start reconnecting with people you know, make new connections and grow your professional network by at least five people (or one new person a week). Attend a networking meeting this month. Get more organized by acquiring a contact management system.

Week #1: Reach out to one person in your network every day via phone, e-mail, or social media. Complete five touch points this first week. Schedule a date to meet one person for coffee or lunch within the next two weeks.

Week #2: Dive deeper into LinkedIn and other social media sites. Review the connections of the people to whom you are linked. Find someone on their list of contacts whom you'd like to meet, and use the system to request an introduction. When you find people you already know, but have not yet linked up to, send them a personal invitation to link in. Do this once daily and accumulate five or more new contacts.

Week #3: Attend a local networking meeting, either as a member or as a guest of a member. Groups to consider include your local chamber of commerce, BNI group, or community service groups (Soroptimist, Rotary, Civitan). If your company hosts onsite meetings for specialty groups, such as Toastmasters, women's alliance, or other special interest groups, consider attending and introducing yourself. Bring plenty of business cards, and go with the intention of making three to five new connections that you will follow up with.

Week #4: Follow up with the leads and connections you made last week. Add these new people to your contact management system. If you need administrative help to get this done and it really isn't your forte, hire an assistant to set it up for you and update it. It is critical that you develop an organized and efficient system that works for you. Do this early, and it will make your networking life a whole lot easier and more fun.

3rd Month: Desired outcomes: Start investing more time and energy into your Top 50 contacts and strengthening those relationships. Continue to add new connections to your professional network. Attend another networking meeting this month. Get serious about follow-up. Demonstrate consistency with daily visits to your preferred social networking media site.

Week #1: Touch base with 10 people from your Top 50 contact list, and strive to add value to their day. Ask them how you can help them, and tell them whom you are looking to meet specifically. Think of whom you could connect your Top 50 people with, and help to facilitate the introductions. "Share an update" on LinkedIn by listing one key thing you are working on right now. Add, do, or change something with your social media account.

Week #2: Continue with your Top 50 outreach. Check-in daily with social media. Schedule networking coffee or lunch with a new contact within the next two weeks. Attend a networking meeting and make three to five new connections. Add these folks to your contact management system.

Week #3: Top 50 outreach. Check in daily to social media. Follow up on the connections that you made last week. Send them an e-mail or handwritten note. Invite them to join your online network through LinkedIn or Facebook. Offer to introduce them to other people in your network who you think would make a good connection. Facilitate that introduction.

Week #4: Top 50 Contact outreach. Check in daily with social media. Find interesting articles, blogs, books, or other content that you think would be valuable to selected people in your network, read them yourself, and then forward them to selected people in your network (via social media, e-mail or snail mail). Ask for their feedback on the content. Engage them in a dialogue, and encourage them to share this information with others in their network that would benefit from it.

Building Momentum

When you bring together focus, motivation, and a solid action plan, any goal is achievable. I encourage you to plot your own course for networking success. With every day and every week that goes by that you are "doing it," you will find it becomes easier, more natural, and infinitely more successful for you. In no time at all, you will build your networking confidence and competence. The professional network that you build will become one of your strongest and most powerful assets.

In the next section you will cruise through eight networking tips featured in my award-winning blog series, "Networking How-To," I selected these specific tips as I find myself sharing them over and over with my clients and audiences. They are simple yet powerfully effectively. By implementing some or all of these ideas, you will boost your networking performance.

> *"Success is not determined by your results. It's determined by your momentum. Your momentum is determined by how you feel. And how you feel is determined by the consistent, daily application of the best you have within you, or your personal best."*
> — MARK LEBLANC, BUSINESS DEVELOPMENT COACH, SPEAKER, AND AUTHOR

27. Fuel Extenders

Tips and Tricks for Greater Mileage in Networking

There are products on the market today that claim they can extend your fuel mileage, reduce your emissions, and renew the life of your engine—all without having to buy a hybrid car. The claims sound great, but few people buy. We live in a skeptical world and we are creatures of habit. Some might call us downright lazy.

Your professional network, much like your car, is a machine with a limited warranty. You take for granted that it will keep running for you, and most of us just like to "gas and go." When it breaks down, we get angry and blame the manufacturer. But somewhere deep down, we know that the buck stops with us. We own the car, after all, and it's up to us to take care of it. It is of our making if we run it into the ground and neglect its maintenance.

The same can be said for your professional network. You don't have to be a mechanic or an expert to look after what you have and to ensure that it runs smoothly for you for a very long time. There are resources that are readily available to you right now to help you maintain your professional network and get greater mileage and a better ride from it. You will need to take action and make some investment in order to benefit from these great networking fuel extenders.

In this next section, you'll read about some of the networking tips that I shared on the blog that accompanied the launch of the first edition of this book. My "Networking How-To" weekly blog posts became very popular amongst my readers, and eventually landed me with the 2014 Best Blog of the Year award by the Women in Business and the Professions World Awards. I've cherry picked a few of the blog topics that I think are the most creative and easiest to implement. In my networking practice, these simple actions have made a material difference in building relationships, landing new business, and having more fun. I encourage you to experiment with a few and assess your results. Modify the techniques to fit your networking engine.

Networking How-To: Nudge

When someone promises to help you out in networking (perhaps connecting you to someone else), they may need a gentle reminder to actually act on their promise and get it done. They may need a little nudge.

No one sets out to be unreliable, but life has a way of getting in the way and we have all become overly distracted (especially with all of these fancy electronic devices at our disposal). Dropping the ball on our promises is one of the pitfalls in networking.

Nudging is essentially follow-up. It is the one of the distinguishing skill sets of an effective networker, and also a successful person. All of us need to be nudged from time to time to remind us of what we need to do...including what we promised you.

You can help people to help you achieve your networking goals if you learn to effectively nudge. You can also request that others nudge you, if you don't respond in a timely manner. Nudging, if done well, can be very helpful indeed.

- Read the entire blog post at www.americasmarketingmotivator. com/networking-how-to-nudge

Networking How-To: Arrive Early

In networking, the early bird gets the worm. So go ahead, show up early on purpose. Arriving early to meetings, presentations, and networking events can give you a unique opportunity to connect and converse with important people that otherwise you might have a difficult time meeting with.

Arrive early for the express purpose of meeting and conversing with new people. This networking tip could save you months of time trying to meet business connections through your regular channels and strategies.

Take a look at your calendar this week. Note the meetings, presentations, and events you are scheduled to attend. Do some quick research to see who else is going to be at the meeting. Is there someone on that list that you'd like to have time with? Select one event this week and mark your calendar to arrive 30-45 minutes early to this meeting.

When you arrive early to the networking event, do not busy yourself with your digital device. Instead, look around to see who you can start a conversation with. Check out the name badges that are laid out on the registration table. See if there is anyone you know or want to meet. You might also offer to help the meeting organizers. Or offer to help with greeting the guests as they arrive. Be the first to welcome them and to shake their hands.

- Read the entire blog post at americasmarketingmotivator.com/networking-how-to-arrive-early

Networking How-To: Rideshare

Ridesharing is not only good for the environment (save on gas and ease up on traffic), it's good for your business relationships and networking opportunities. Commuting to events can go from being a time waster to a relationship builder. Time in transit together is time well spent. At least that has been my experience.

Find out who else is going to this same networking event and ask them to join you in your car. That's right, you initiate a rideshare invitation. Not only will this commitment ensure that you show up for the event (i.e. someone is counting on you), but you will advance a strategic relationship, either with a colleague, client, or new connection.

If you are at a conference, consider sharing a taxi or offering a lift to someone who is also going to the airport or nearby hotel. Make sure you exchange business cards and follow up with them when you get home. I suggest sending them a LinkedIn invitation and a personal note or e-mail, or making a phone call a few days later to say how much you enjoyed getting to know them.

- Read the entire blog post at americasmarketingmotivator.com/ networking-how-to-rideshare

> *When you adopt a relationship-based networking practice, your mindset shifts from scarcity to abundance.*

Networking How-To: Collaborate with Competitors

When you adopt a relationship-based networking practice, your mindset shifts from scarcity to abundance. You come to believe that there is enough opportunity out there for everyone. This means that the people you normally view as your competitors could become advocates, connections, and even friends.

But sports and politics have trained us that someone has to win, while the other loses. That's the way we have defined the game. There can be only one team that wins the Super Bowl and only one athlete that takes home the Olympic gold medal per event. Only one person wins the Presidency. The other person is the loser. They are forgotten by the public. It's a sad outcome faced by many star athletes and politicians.

But in contrast to sport and politics, the goal in business is to create as much value for as many people as possible. Businesses also want that value to last for as long as possible, not just for the immediate moment. I believe that collaboration is a fundamental part of winning in business and in life.

By adopting a collaborative mindset, you too can enjoy many benefits in your business and your career, not the least of which is growing your sphere of influence, gaining referral partners, and becoming more valuable to your clients as you can confidently refer work that doesn't hit your sweet spot.

In my opinion, it's more fun to collaborate than to compete with others. So get to know and network with your "competitors." They may end up becoming your good friends and professional colleagues.

- Read the entire blog post at americasmarketingmotivator.com/networking-how-to-collaborate-with-competitors

Networking How-To: Tap into Spousal Influence

Everyone you meet in the networking process has a uniquely different network than yours. If you are effective at building trust and connection with them, they might just open up their network to you. The largest value of this new connection may lie not in the person in front of you, but the people that they connect you to—their people—and that includes their spousal partner.

There are fewer connections as strong as married couples. They live together, sleep together, eat together, and hopefully love each other. Spouses have influence over and equity with each other. If one of them likes you and wants to help you in networking, they may be talking about you to their spouse at home. Let's hope it's positive talk.

Spousal influence has helped me clinch job offers, secure agreement on new business proposals, and has allowed me to connect with and help more people. And yes, make more friends.

When you are networking with other people this week, be sure to include the question, "What does your spouse/partner do for a living?" If the spouse is a stay-at-home mom/dad, inquire what interests and organizations he/she belongs to. Consider the possibility of how you could help your contact's spouse through your network and resources. Share information about your spouse/partner when you network. Be on the look out for new connections for your better half. For your closer contacts, consider doing a couples dinner outing or inviting them over to your home for a meal. Get to know the partner in addition to your original networking contact. This could enrich and extend your sphere of influence and allow you to deepen your relationships.

- Read the entire blog post at americasmarketingmotivator.com/ networking-how-to-tap-into-spousal-influence

Networking How-To: Take a Seat at the Table

I believe that it is important that you are not only seen, but also heard at networking events and business meetings. Don't diminish yourself by hiding or taking an obscure seat far away from others. Have the courage to select a seat near someone you want to meet. Don't stay in your comfort zone by sitting with people you already know. Be bold and sit with new people (yes, strangers) and learn to start conversations.

If you are attending a networking meeting where you'll be seated at a table, I suggest you follow these three rules for table meetings:

- **Rule #1:** Select a seat where you can be seen and heard

- **Rule #2:** When appropriate, speak up so that your ideas will be heard

- **Rule #3:** Only speak when you are looking at a pair of eyes

Arrive early to the next networking event or business meeting. Observe the room and decide strategically where the best place is for you: that is, the space that will give you the most exposure and opportunity. Take it. Claim it. Own your personal power. Don't sit by yourself at an empty table hoping that others might join you. Don't allow your fear or self-doubt to relegate you to the passive positions in the room. Step up, stand out, and let your voice be heard. Take your seat at the table. Make it a good seat that allows you to make powerful connections.

- Read the entire blog post at americasmarketingmotivator.com/ networking-how-to-take-a-seat-at-the-table

Networking How-To: Create a Lending Library

How many business books do you have on your bookshelf at home? Or if you are a digital book reader, think about the books that have made a material difference in your thinking? How about recommending, loaning, or even gifting some of these inspiring resources to people in your network? As simple as it sounds, sharing books is a great networking tip. Why? Because it allows you to help others with resources you already have. It declutters your home/office, by moving out book inventory. I like to put my name inside the books under the header "Pass It On." I envision others following my example, adding their name and then the book to another person. Being able to see who has touched this book before you adds value and interest to the reader. I believe loaning or gifting a book from your personal library is even more valuable than buying your contact a brand new book. Why? Because you can sign it, slip in your business card, and add that personal touch. They might even benefit from reading your crib notes in the side margins. This book is part of you and by lending or gifting it, you are sharing part of you with someone else. To save some money on shipping costs, check to see if the post office in your area offers a 'Media Mail' lower rate for sending books. If you want your book back, make that very clear to the recipient at the outset of the loan. This creates an obligation, and another reason to get in touch with each other in the near future. That creates networking opportunity. So go ahead, pass it on. Create a lending library to help you enhance your networking relationships.

- Read the entire blog post at americasmarketingmotivator.com/ networking-how-to-create-a-lending-library

Networking How-To: Schedule a Three-Way Lunch

Think about the many people that you have wanted to connect with. Perhaps you sent an e-mail introduction or tried to connect with them on LinkedIn. You never know if they will act upon your introduction. People are busy and reluctant. They miss out on the potential opportunity that you see in this new connection. How can you make sure it happens? Schedule a three-way lunch. By doing this, you know that it will happen, because you'll be there to witness it. Yes, it takes more administrative time and effort. (Don't you hate trying to coordinate three calendars?) Yes, it will cost you more money. No, you are not babysitting. You are witnessing the power of being a conduit of people. And while your intention is to help two people help each other, you will find that opportunity and good will are created for you too. As a networking practice, I try to schedule a three-way lunch at least once per quarter. They are fun, they are effective, and they are good practice. Give it a try.

- Read the entire blog post at americasmarketingmotivator.com/ networking-how-to-schedule-a-three-way-lunch

I hope these fuel-extending tips and ideas will be useful to you in getting the most out of your networking efforts. But let's turn the page and ground ourselves in the higher purpose of networking. What it's really all about.

> "If you want to go fast, go alone. If you want to go far, go together."
> — AFRICAN PROVERB

28. The Road Less Taken

The Journey to a More Rewarding Career,
Business, and Life

As we come to the end of the third edition of this book, I am inspired to call upon the profound works of two amazing thought-leaders: the poet Robert Frost, and M. Scott Peck, psychiatrist and best-selling author.

Robert Frost's poem *The Road Not Taken*, published in 1916, speaks to the tough choices people have to make when traveling the road of life. Inevitably, you have to leave some possibilities unexplored as you make choices and move forward in your career and life. Wouldn't it be great if we could do it all, experience it all, have it all? The exciting news is that networking expands your possibilities as you amass and carry with you a growing number of mutually beneficial relationships to support you on your life's journey. It is limited only by the time, energy, and commitment that you put into it.

Dr. Peck's profound book *The Road Less Traveled* was first published in 1978, but didn't become a best-seller until 1984, some six years after he hit the lecture circuit and personally sought reviews in key publications (now there's a testament to persistence and personal conviction). If you haven't read this amazing personal manifesto for living, I suggest you pick it up and read it. His insights on the value of discipline and its connection to our emotional, spiritual, and psychological health can also be applied to the health of our professional and business lives. He outlines in depth why the ability to delay gratification is good for us, a character trait that has significantly waned with the daily advancements in technology. His commentary on accepting responsibility for oneself and one's own actions continues to be highly relevant and needed in our world. This is perhaps the essential starting point for individual empowerment and real change. Playing the blame game and living with excuses will never get you very far or make you truly happy.

These philosophies of living are precisely the qualities that will make you more successful in your business and professional life—discipline, patience, personal responsibility, authenticity, and positive intention. Integrating these philosophies into your daily working habits will enrich your relationships in every sphere of your life.

I'd like to share three final examples of meaningful connections that were born out of networking. These relationships have brought enormous joy, enrichment, and opportunity to me, both personally and professionally. If you examine your own life, you might find you have similar examples of how networking has blessed your life.

Networking Magic

I often refer to networking as "magic." I look for and celebrate networking magic whenever I see it in my own life or in other people's lives. Last week, I reflected on a bit of networking magic that had touched my own life. It all started with my connection to Marge Piccini. When we first met, both Marge and I were new entrepreneurs, venturing into the world of small business, with big hopes and dreams. We seemed to move in similar circles and have shared contacts, so it made sense to get to know each other better. After returning from a business conference in San Francisco, Marge called me to say that she had met one of the instructors and purchased his audio program. She had a sense that I would like it, so she loaned it to me. This was my first introduction to Arthur Samuel Joseph, the founder of the Vocal Awareness Institute. This simple act of networking kindness by Marge opened up a whole new world of personal and professional growth for me.

After listening to Arthur's audio program, *Voice of a Leader,* I was intrigued. I ordered his book, *Vocal Power,* and consumed it. Then I ordered his next book, *Vocal Leadership*, and underlined a significant number of passages. I began purchasing his books and audio programs and gifting them to my clients, friends, and networking connections. Certainly, I become a fan of Arthur's work.

Then I took a risk. I sent Arthur a LinkedIn invitation with a personal note. Shockingly, he responded. (Note: now that I know Arthur, it is not shocking that he would do the respectful and professional thing and respond to someone who reached out to him.). Since that time, our connection has grown. I hired Arthur as my vocal coach and completed a number of coaching sessions. I then invited Arthur to collaborate with me on a client project. This allowed us to further our connection by becoming professional colleagues and partners. Then I asked Arthur for a big favor. I asked him to write the foreword to my book, *Stop Global Boring*. He replied with a responding YES, letting me know it wasn't a favor, but an honor for him to do so. Every encounter that I have with Arthur Samuel Joseph lifts me up and encourages me to "Be My Self." He has helped me to be a more inspiring person committed to excellence and integrity in the Work (with a capital W as he likes to say). Arthur has helped me share my Work with more people in more powerful ways.

When I look back on the chain of events that led to me building a relationship with this profound thought-leader, I am in awe. It was truly a bit of networking magic that blessed both of our lives. I will be eternally grateful to Marge Piccini for introducing me to Arthur Samuel Joseph and his work.

If you commit to studying the art of networking and applying its techniques, tools, and attitudes, you will quickly find yourself on an exciting new journey that you won't ever want to end.

Friends for Life

I experienced another bit of networking magic in a phone conversation with a professional colleague, David O'Brien. David is a leadership consultant, speaker, author, and business owner of WorkChoice Solutions, LLC. David has referred me to several of his clients, and as a result, I've landed new business and generated more income. David started the conversation by thanking me for being my wonderful self (as he put it), for doing excellent work, for taking great care of his clients, and for being a good friend. The sincerity in his voice and the words he chose to express himself warmed my heart. I knew that there would be many other positive moments and new opportunities in our future as we had both invested in our relationship.

How did I meet David? I met him several years ago through another networking connection, Nancy Anton. And you guessed it, I met Nancy through another professional friend who felt we just had to meet because it was a "natural connection." She was right. My connection with Nancy was immediate and profound. Our relationship has led to many career, business, and life enhancements for us both. And of course, we have introduced each other to other great people, like David.

As I reflect on these two relationships—Nancy Anton and David O'Brien—I am reminded that they both started out in the "strangers" category. Over time, these relationships progressed deeper down the "Networking Funnel of Opportunity" (see Chapter 14) until they reached the last level—the ultimate level: life-long friendship. I feel blessed and honored to call Nancy and David my friends, in addition to my professional colleagues. It is my intention to remain friends with them for many years to come. I love these two individuals and would do anything for them. That's the power of networking. That's the ultimate prize in my book.

Larger Purpose

Let me share one final example of the profound impact that networking can have on your life and those around you. I recently attended a large scale fundraising luncheon for the YWCA Hartford Region. Their annual "In the Company of Women" luncheon attracts over 1,300 philanthropic women and men to the convention center in Hartford, Connecticut. I have been a table captain for many years, recruiting friends to join me at this event in order to help raise more money and more supporters. I have also served on the board of directors of this nonprofit organization for more than six years. My involvement has been an incredible professional and personal development experience, and it has allowed me to meet and build relationships with some incredible people who I might not have otherwise ever met.

As I walked around the ballroom crowded with people and filled with enthusiasm, I was struck once again by the power of networking. I hugged more people that day than I do in a typical month. I was able to introduce and connect other people who might benefit from knowing each other. And we were all there to marshal our collective resources and energy to help the YWCA Hartford fulfill its mission of eliminating racism and empowering women. It is because we come together and connect with a shared passion for helping others that we are able to make greater things happen.

Some of you might think that I'm talking about philanthropy, or development, or charity. But really, I am talking about the power of networking. We have the ability to share our social capital to make our communities better places in which to live and work. We network, connect, and genuinely want to help others. And in doing so, we help ourselves. We mobilize our network for the greater good. When we network, we are participating in something larger than ourselves. Who wouldn't want to be part of that?

The Road to Mutually Beneficial Relationships

Throughout this book, we have discussed that networking is essentially the art of building and sustaining mutually beneficial relationships before you need them. It is a win-win-win game. It takes energy, motivation, and discipline to play the networking game well. And it can be tons of fun in the process. If you commit to studying the art of networking and applying its techniques, tools and attitudes into your daily life, you will quickly find yourself on an exciting new journey that you won't ever want to end. The destination stop-offs will be rewarding and memorable, and you will want to go back for more and more.

You can never outgrow networking, never be too young or too old to do it, use it, and enjoy it. It is an ageless, timeless, professional skill, if not an essential life skill. It will help you get where you want to go.

Networking is a Strategy for a Successful Life

Some of you reading this book did so to solve a real and immediate problem, such as unemployment, the desire to land a better job, launching a new business, or securing your next client. Your motivation to apply the networking skills that you've learned in this book is clear and compelling. I encourage you to go for it. Try it out. Put those ideas into practice now, and measure your success. Leverage networking to achieve your next goal.

I also want to encourage you to go beyond that immediate short-term goal. I invite you to continue on the journey of building long-term relationships for the rest of your life; to permanently alter your personal definition of networking from an event or an activity that you have to do at certain times in your work life to a core strategy for creating a successful career, business, and life for yourself and others whom you care about. I invite you to join me and become a motivated networker.

Enjoy the ride.

Kathy McAfee

America's Marketing Motivator

> "I took the one less traveled by, and that has made all the difference."
>
> — EXCERPT FROM *THE ROAD NOT TAKEN* BY ROBERT FROST

Final Checklist #4

Congratulations! You've arrived. You've completed all four parts of this book. You have acquired the networking skills and confidence to practice the following beliefs and behaviors:

☐ I can confidently work a room, starting and ending conversations with ease. I can mingle without feeling awkward and regularly practice the "be the host" networking technique.

☐ I am a connector of people and actively practice putting people and ideas together, even if it doesn't benefit me directly. I see beyond myself.

☐ I consider myself to be a student of networking, constantly seeking out new information and new experiences in order to enhance my mastery of the art of networking. I teach others what I have learned.

☐ I am strategic and thoughtful in my approach to networking. I have a road map and action plan to guide me to my desired destination in business and in life.

☐ I actively seek to increase my sphere of influence by networking with people of greater power, influence, and resources than I currently have. I know that I too can bring value to these new networking relationships. Together, we can create greater value and more opportunities for ourselves and others in the world.

☐ I understand that networking is not an event or an activity, but a strategy for life. It has become an integral part of how I conduct business, how I manage my career, and how I guide my life.

Index

Networking Ahead by Kathy McAfee

About the Author

Kathy McAfee is an executive presentation coach and professional speaker, and is known as America's Marketing Motivator. Her mission is to help corporate leaders, business professionals, entrepreneurs, engineers, job seekers, and college students to more effectively use their talent, energy, and influence to create positive changes in the world.

She is the author of two books, *Stop Global Boring*, and *Networking Ahead*. She is also the recipient of the prestigious Best Blog of the Year, as awarded by The Women in Business and The Professions World Awards (2014).

In her role as executive presentation coach, she helps clients increase their confidence, credibility, and influence by reducing their PowerPoint clutter to better engage their audiences and move them to action. A certified Master Practitioner of Neuro Linguistic Programming (NLP), Kathy shows her clients how to clear their limiting beliefs and use more effective strategies to realize their full leadership potential.

Over 30 years, Kathy has succeeded in numerous corporate leadership positions. She's brought marketing success to major organizations including Levi Strauss & Co., Maybelline, Southcorp Wines of Australia, and ADVO. On a three-year assignment in England, Kathy led European marketing initiatives for an international vision care company. In 2005, Kathy gave flight to her entrepreneurial dreams and launched Kmc Brand Innovation, LLC, a talent development company offering communication training, executive and business coaching, and keynote speaking services to her motivated clients.

Kathy is a graduate of Stanford University in Economics. She is a member of the National Speakers Association, a past board member for the YWCA of the Hartford Region, and an active member of Soroptimist International of the Americas. A resilient woman, Kathy is also an ovarian cancer survivor, and holds a second degree black belt in the martial art of Tae Kwon Do. Kathy and her husband Byron, along with their dog and three cats reside in the beautiful state of South Carolina.

Contact Information:

Kathy McAfee
Executive Presentation Coach and Professional Speaker

Website: AmericasMarketingMotivator.com

Telephone: (860) 371-8801

E-mail: Kathy@AmericasMarketingMotivator.com

Social Media:

 LinkedIn profile:linkedin.com/in/kathymcafee

 Subscribe to her channel: youtube.com/user/ kathymcafee

 Facebook: www.facebook.com/NetworkingAhead

Instagram: instagram.com/ kathymcafeemarketingmotivator/

Learn more about Kathy's business, visit her web site:
AmericasMarketingMotivator.com

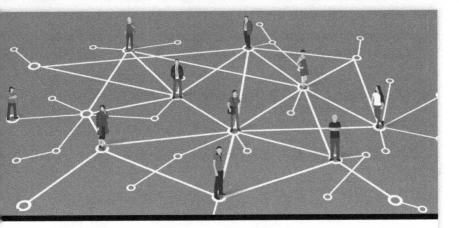

TAKE YOUR TALENT TO THE NEXT LEVEL

with Kathy McAfee
America's Marketing Motivator

Scan this QR Code
with your mobile device
to receive networking tips
and career wisdom delivered
straight to your inbox

Or go online to:
www.americasmarketingmotivator.com/#signup

Unleash the Power of Connection

If you like what you've read, consider partnering with Kathy McAfee on one (or more) of her programs and services:

For Corporate Diversity & Inclusion Programs

- **Instructional seminars and presentations.** Members of your organization's women's network, and other diversity groups, will benefit from Kathy's motivating programs, including *Networking Ahead for Your Career*, *ExecConnect*, *Presenting Your Professional Best*, and *Stop Global Boring*. Participants will increase their confidence and become more effective in making new connections, advocating for others, positioning themselves for new opportunities, and building strategic relationships.

For Organizations' Talent Development Programs

- **Emerging Leader Programs.** Enrich your high-potential talent development initiative by training your future leaders in the art of advanced networking, communication, and influence. Ask about Kathy's signature training program: *The Motivated Presenter*.

- **Professional Development Classes.** Through her half-day and full-day skill-building classes, Kathy will help your associates build their spheres of influence inside and outside your organization – empowering them to take greater ownership of their career paths, serve as ambassadors for your organization, and assist with new business development.

- **New Hire Orientation Programs.** Help your new employees successfully navigate your organization by including a networking skills class as part of your onboarding program. Kathy will help you fast track new hire success by building greater camaraderie, connection, and engagement.

- **Lunch and Lead Motivating Seminars.** Kathy will facilitate a lively and instructive discussion with your team on networking, personal branding, communication, or presentation skills. (60-90 minutes: in-person or virtual)

- **Virtual Learning.** Kathy will host an online series tailored for your needs which will feature customized, actionable content delivered by a range of motiving, high-engagement experts.

Take Your Talent to the Next Level

For Conferences & Meetings

- **Motivational keynote speaking.** Kathy speaks on a number of professional topics including networking, communication mastery, women's empowerment, personal branding, leadership, and surviving cancer. Conference participants will be inspired by her personal stories and energy. They will be engaged by her speed networking exercises to make more meaningful connections. Kathy is also available to serve as a break out session facilitator, panelist, panel moderator, or emcee.

For Entrepreneurs & Business Owners

- Kathy offers one-on-one coaching programs (virtual or in-person) that will accelerate business development through enhanced networking, communication and sales strategies.

For College Students

- **Networking on Purpose.** Kathy teaches and motivates college students to pre-launch their careers by learning to build their professional networks now. Young people will practice networking skills including how to start a conversation, participate in an effective interview, and build their digital presence.

Contact Kathy McAfee

 (860) 371.8801

 Kathy@AmericasMarketingMotivator.com

Learn more at:

http://www.americasmarketingmotivator.com/services/

CPSIA information can be obtained
at www.ICGtesting.com
Printed in the USA
BVHW03s0605120918
527258BV00001B/1/P